CULTURE
SHOCK

SURVIVING
FIVE GENERATIONS
IN ONE WORKPLACE

By Joanna Dodd Massey, Ph.D.

Culture Shock: Surviving Five Generations in One Workplace

Front Book Cover Design by Gian Colombo

Design Graphic Consultant for TVGuestpert Publishing by Jonathan Fong

Book Design by Carole Allen Design Studio

Author Photos by Stephanie Simpson, Simpson Portraits

Edited by TVGuestpert Publishing

Published by TVGuestpert Publishing

11664 National Blvd, #345
Los Angeles, CA. 90064
310-584-1504
www.TVGuestpertPublishing.com
www.TVGuestpert.com
First Printing May 2020
10 9 8 7 6 5 4 3 2 1

JOANNA DODD MASSEY, PHD

CULTURE
SHOCK

SURVIVING
FIVE GENERATIONS
IN ONE WORKPLACE

Table of Contents

DEDICATION

To my mother, Barbara Massey, for all of her love and support, and for the incredible example she sets for me as a classy, ethical, loyal and successful Silent Generation businesswoman.

ACKNOWLEDGMENTS

I have to start by thanking my mother, as well as my father, who passed away when I was 17. Thanks to everything they provided for me—from the opportunities I was given as a kid growing up in New York City to my education—I have been given advantages in life that helped shape who I am, and I am grateful for all of it.

Thank you to my dear friend Jacquie Jordan, whose calm and clear-headed direction got me through writer's block many times. I am grateful for the help I received from Jacquie and her amazing team of professional writers, editors, publishers and marketers at TVGuestpert, who helped structure the book and guide it in the best way. Thank you also to Melissa Grego for writing the Foreword, and to Paige Adams-Geller and Lisa Gooder for their back-cover endorsements. Lisa and I met in prep school; Paige and I went to college together; and Melissa and I began working with each other in the 1990s. All of them are inspirational, successful business women, whom I admire and adore.

There are three people I want to thank for their invaluable behind-the-scenes help. Jordan Massey and Michaela Sell conducted research for the book. Jordan also served as my assistant during the research panel with Generation Alpha. Gian Colombo is the genius designer who makes everything my company does look good, from our website to our corporate decks and, most especially, the cover of this book.

I received very helpful guidance on some of the more challenging topics in this book from three key people. The first is Rebecca Ascher-Walsh, one of my oldest and dearest friends. Rebecca is a brilliant journalist, author and a lifelong sage, who has been my personal cheerleader since we were six years old. The second is my ex-husband Brian Lowry, a journalist with impeccable ethics, who looked at the book with a protective eye as he guided me toward keeping it fair and balanced without tipping too far in either direction. Hopefully, I was able to take his notes and artfully create that balance—the readers will certainly let me know whether or not I did. The third is Joe Flint, also a noted journalist, who provided invaluable input delivered with his signature candor, which I appreciate.

Thank you also to three of my Chapin sisters—Stephanie Simpson, Vanessa McGrady and Andrea Sluchan, who confidently encouraged me on my path, which is something they have been doing since we were in grammar school.

There are many colleagues who either shaped my career or served as teachers, which enabled me to become an expert in America's youth. (This list is in a chronological order that probably only makes sense to me.) A big thank you to Dawn Ostroff, Sahar Elhabashi, Croi McNamara, Teal Newland, Libby Duke, Azadeh Rongère, Jon Feltheimer, Michael Burns, Ross Pollack, Peter Wilkes, Cristina Castañeda, Margaret Loesch, Dan Pimentel, Rick Haskins, Leslie Moonves, Nancy Tellem, Gil Schwartz, Chris Ender, Dean Valentine, and Eric Schotz.

I would also like to thank some of the professors who had a big impact on me during my path to Ph.D. Their wisdom and teachings gave me a deep understanding of human psychology and relationship dynamics, which help me as a leader and an executive. Thank you, Dr. Genie Palmer, Dr. Mark Allan Kaplan, Dr. Marvin D. Seppala, Dr. Victor Cohen, Dr. Joy Turek, and Thomas Mondragon, LMFT.

Finally, I would like to thank some friends and teachers who have supported and influenced me on my winding road. Thank you, Amanda Cooper, Siddiqi Soul Ray, Anne Alene, Therese McDonough, Jordan Marinov, Bobbi Thompson, Terri Cole Elston, Jenny Davidson-Goldbronn, Camilla Outzen Rantsen, Elaine Fintel, Sarah Scheper, Kelly Shemonis and J.G.

EDITORIAL NOTE

I follow the Associated Press Stylebook when it comes to writing. The AP Stylebook is the bible for newspaper journalists and PR people when it comes to formal writing. The Stylebook covers rules about everything—from whether or not to include the state after a reference to a smaller city, and using quotes or italics for the name of a movie, to comma usage, and when you are supposed to capitalize certain words. Along those lines, AP Stylebook says that all generational names are lower case, except for Generation X, because that is the title of a book. It also says you capitalize references to Generation Z. No good explanation given.

You know what? It looks wrong to lowercase some of the generation names and not all of them. So, I use capitals throughout the book. If you catch a reference to a generational name in lower case somewhere in this book, it is because my copy editor and I missed it!

I know most of you will not care about this but, for those who pay attention to details like that, I felt the need to explain it.

FOREWORD

As the CEO of the Hollywood Radio and Television Society (HRTS), I have a front-row seat to the massive shifts that are happening in culture and business now that Millennials and Generation Z have entered the workforce. HRTS is a business association and the companies represented among our membership include the television networks, studios and streamers that are on the frontlines of the changes, since they create content for and employ a lot of young adults.

Prior to joining HRTS, I was a journalist covering the media industry, so Joanna and I have known each other for most of our careers. I know that she didn't set out to become a generational expert, but she spent her career focused on youth and youth culture, so it makes perfect sense to me that she embraced that expertise and incorporated it into her career trajectory.

Joanna and I have a lot in common, which is probably why we are now friends. We are both female executives who have been willing to take risks as we pivot our careers in new and exciting ways. We support each other in those pivots, which is why I am honored to write the Foreword to her book.

Joanna has worked for many of the most influential media companies in the United States—CBS, Viacom, Lionsgate, Discovery, Hasbro, and Condé Nast. She has held senior communications positions at multiple networks and production studios. As a result, she has been on the forefront of digital content distribution and viewing since the 1990s, when it first became a possibility.

While she spent nearly 30 years at traditional media companies, she was fortunate to work in a part of the media business dedicated to targeting youth and making sure they could see content whenever and wherever they wanted. Like the advertisers on Madison Avenue, Hollywood executives strive to accurately reflect youth culture and to reach young adults between 18 and 34 years old. Since it is a creative business, they tend to employ young people in order to tap into the cultural zeitgeist of the times. That's how Joanna formed her expertise in promoting to and working with Millennials and Gen Z.

Most people think of PR executives as those who work with the press and communicate important messages about the company to key constituents, such as consumers and investors. However, the Chief Communications Officer is also responsible for internal communications between executives and employees. Joanna works closely with the CEO and Chief Human Resources Officer on all communications that go to employees. This trifecta of C-suite executives is responsible for ensuring the company can attract the best talent in the market and retain them to avoid a high turnover in staff.

She has also managed younger employees her entire career. Over coffee recently, Joanna told me that as the head of communications for Condé Nast Entertainment and a member of the Senior Staff, she was among the five oldest people in a division of 300 employees—and she was not yet 50 years old at that time. Moreover, the staff members in her department were all under the age of 30.

I think this topic is fascinating and, during our coffee date, I grilled her about the book and her work as a corporate speaker. I asked her, "How do you translate what's happening for your audiences so they can glean practical tools to navigate all of these changes?"

Her response was eye opening, as she laid out the following scenario for me: "Let's say you're having a debate in the office about the procurement of paper and boxes. If you're talking to someone from the Silent Generation, consider that they grew up during the Depression and, when they were kids, they had to carefully unwrap their gifts, so they could reuse the paper and boxes for the next birthday, because there was a shortage of materials, as well as money to buy them. Maybe you're talking to a Gen Xer, who was brought up during the excess of the 1980s when they tore open gifts and threw away the paper and boxes—in extra-large plastic garbage bags. Or maybe it's a Gen Zer, who has existential angst about using paper and boxes because of the harm it does to the environment."

The person's experiences growing up are going to automatically dictate their perceptions and reactions. Understanding people will make YOU more effective at dealing with those differences. It's also helpful to the other person, because when we feel understood, our defenses go down; we are more open to different ideas and to change."

It was a simple example that perfectly illustrated the miscommunications we are experiencing at work every day.

Between her doctorate degree in psychology, MBA and 25-year career as a communications executive at major media companies, Joanna is the perfect person to translate for a broad audience the issues we are experiencing with all of these generations in the workforce for the first time.

I'm so thankful that she has done this work and is game to share it with us all. The learning Joanna has packed into CULTURE SHOCK represents a huge opportunity for readers to gain an edge and an understanding of how to work better with everyone around us no matter our generation. That goes for those just starting out, well on our way, and even the most experienced professionals among us.

Melissa Grego
CEO, Hollywood Radio & Television Society

CULTURE EATS STRATEGY FOR BREAKFAST |
A NOTE FROM THE AUTHOR

There is a popular quote right now, "Culture eats strategy for breakfast." It means that your company can have a kickass strategy that is guaranteed to succeed but, if you have a bad corporate culture, your strategy will fail—and it will fail fast.

There are hard costs to businesses when it comes to workplace well-being. If a company's employees are not happy, that company is losing millions of dollars in worker dissatisfaction and stress. Let the statistics speak for themselves:

- Employees under a lot of stress—whether that stress is due to overwork, lack of good pay to support the family, or a toxic workplace with a lot of gossip and backstabbing—cost companies 40 percent more than the average worker.[1]

- Next is workplace bullying, which is more prevalent than companies realize. The Workplace Bullying Institute defines it as "verbal abuse," "threatening, humiliating or intimidating" and behavior that prevents work from getting done, such as sabotage.[2] Business Insider estimates that bullying, which creates a toxic workplace, can cost a Fortune 500 company $8 million in lost productivity and $100,000 to over $1 million in litigation, plus $16 million in turnover.[3]

- Stress, lack of support and low pay create angry or dissatisfied employees, who will often do unethical things to get back at a company they feel is wronging them. This includes theft, which Business Insider states is 48 percent of the cause for inventory shrinkage. It also includes treating customers badly, which costs untold millions in lost revenue and repeat business.

- A final thought on the hard costs of a problematic workplace culture: It costs 30 to 50 percent of a junior person's salary to replace them. For a mid-level employee, the cost to replace is 150 percent, or 1.5 times their base salary![4]

When I started working in PR and marketing, we did not have cell phones or email at home. When you left the office, you were out of touch until the next day, unless you had an assistant or junior executive working late who could track you down on your home phone or pager. Yes, I started working when dinosaurs roamed the earth. (We even had a dress code: women were mandated to wear skirts and pantyhose or a pant suit. No bare legs allowed and no jeans.)

My first job was in the LA office of the international PR firm Fleishman Hillard. I would get to work at 6:45 a.m., just before my boss, who got in at 7:00 a.m., so I could get face time with her while we went downstairs to get coffee. I feel like I need to make an editorial note here that "face time" back then meant being with someone in person, not talking to them over a phone by video!

I left work every night a few minutes after my boss, usually at 7:30 p.m. I was in the office most weekends wearing business casual, which meant the men did not have to wear a tie, but women basically wore the same thing they wore all week long.

It was the early 1990s and I was in the habit of going to Saturday football games at the Coliseum to cheer on the University of Southern California (USC) in my business clothes. It was at one of those games that I ran into a friend who subsequently got me a job working for CBS. She asked why I was at the football game in business attire and it led to a conversation about changing jobs. Apparently, wearing a business dress to a football game can have a good outcome!

Times have definitely changed. Millennials and Gen Z were brought up by those of us with long-time business perspective, i.e., Gen X (born 1965–1980), Baby Boomers (born 1946–1964) and the Silent Generation (1928–1945). I am talking about people who were in the workforce through the 1960s, 70s, 80s, 90s and early 2000s. The younger generations were raised with different values and boundaries than older generations were given. As a result, they have a very different view of the world and of work.

I am writing this book from the perspective of understanding these younger generations and embracing the changes they are bringing to America. But what gives me that perspective? I wear three different hats as I write this.

The first hat is as a marketer who has spent 30 years promoting products and ideas to 18-to-34-year-old consumers.

The second hat is as a senior communications executive in

the media industry, where creativity and young culture are valued above experience. That means we hire and promote a lot of young people. I benefited from that culture by becoming a Vice President at 29 years old and a Senior Vice President running a bi-coastal staff and a multi-million-dollar P&L by the age of 32. As a leader and manager, I have been hiring and mentoring younger generations for two decades.

The third hat is as a Doctor of Psychology, which provided me with a better understanding of human nature and how people from different backgrounds and generations interact at work.

> **NOTE:** *The psychology degree seemed like a weird left turn in the middle of my career in media. I took a forced break from work when I was downsized right before the recession in 2007 and decided to go back to school to study psychology while I waited out the recession.*
>
> *That idea to go back to school sounded like this: "Hmmm, what should I do while I am out of work for the next few YEARS?! I know, I will get a master's degree in psychology and, if the economy gets better sooner than expected, I will just go back to work!"*
>
> *That thought turned into 11 years of me pursuing graduate degrees. I obtained a master's in clinical psychology from Antioch in Los Angeles; a Ph.D. in transpersonal psychology from a small school called Sofia University in Palo Alto, California; a master's in business administration (MBA) from USC; and a graduate certificate in corporate finance from Harvard. I had full-time jobs for two of the four degrees, which only proves that I am insane and can function on very little sleep.*

Workplace Well-Being Is More Important than Material Benefits

Back in 2015, the Harvard Business Review reported on a study which found that employees preferred "workplace wellbeing [sic] to material benefits."[5] If you think about it, it makes sense. We spend more time at work than we do with our families. People are saying they want to be happy and that is more important to their physical and emotional well-being than how much money they make.

Since 2009—when the economy started to grow after the recession and Millennials began to make an indelible mark on workplace habits—companies started to focus on workplace well-being. Corporate culture became a buzzword. An untold number of academic institutions, corporations and research institutes studied Millennial psychographics—attitudes, opinions, lifestyles and interests—to figure out how to recruit and retain young talent.

The same is now being done for Gen Z. Young people are leaving corporate America in droves. They prefer the gig economy (projects and task jobs) to staff jobs (paid hourly or by salary). The American ideal—the one in which you graduate from school and get a job at a solid company where you work your way up the ladder for the next 4o years is over... so is retiring at the age of 65. More on all of this later in the book.

Some experts are concerned that the current emphasis on culture and workplace well-being will disappear in the next recession, as companies pull back and employees risk losing their jobs and not being able to find other work. At the risk of being accused of not knowing history and sounding like a fool if I am proven wrong, I do not think that is going to happen. People who say that culture will be deemphasized in our next recession are misjudging the values of these younger generations.

Read on and you will find out why!

CHAPTER 1 | THE GENERATIONAL DIVIDE

Millennials get a bad rap for being entitled. I have worked with innumerable Millennials who are self-deprecating about the entitlement trait, as they sheepishly but resolutely ask for more flexibility at work, time off, and/or more perks. Some of them recognize entitlement in their peers, but not in themselves. Still others live up to the entitlement label and embrace it fully. One employee once looked at me as I told her we were all going to have to work over the Christmas holiday and said, "But I need me time."

Okay, here is the truth about that exchange. I agreed with her!

We all need "me time." The Silent Generation, Baby Boomers and Gen X have collectively created a work environment where it is assumed that if you are going to move up the corporate ladder, you will ignore your health, skip the gym, eat greasy food at your desk and work until you get an ulcer, all while missing your 5-year-old's dance recital and your teenager's soccer game. Date night with your significant other is a distant memory to return when you are an empty nester, if you live that long.

When my employee said pleadingly that she needed "me time," I had that familiar defense response that older workers get when faced with a younger employee saying they need and deserve more freedom. In that moment, the voice in my head said to me, "I have worked through every vacation I have taken in the past 25 years… and that started before the Blackberry was invented!"

Fortunately, I have a pause button, thanks to decades of training in psychology and business, so what came out of my mouth was, "I understand. And we will all get more me time once this project is done… and a heck of a lot more of it if the event doesn't go well and the CEO fires us. Let's work out a compromise where you don't spend your whole vacation reacting whenever we call, but instead you put in an hour or two each morning and send us a daily update on your portion of the project. We will only email if we have a question that needs to be answered immediately. Also, we can put 'urgent' in the subject line in those cases."

As a member of Generation X, I know that I am not the only person who gets annoyed or defensive when a Millennial employee tells us they need more responsibility, autonomy, and freedom to come and go as they please. Colleagues have shared with me their frustration: "That's not fair. I put in my time, now they need to put in theirs!" Or, "They haven't earned it yet." Or, "When they're the senior person with the corner office, they can decide who gets me time, but for now, just do the damn job."

Okay, yes, we did put in our time and so did the Baby Boomers and the Silent Generation, but that defensive reaction does not help the situation. In fact, it causes a divide in business that creates friction and misunderstanding in the workplace. That in turn leads to lost productivity and contributes to a toxic work culture, which can damage your company's reputation, increase your business risk with employees who are not engaged or happy, and ultimately lead to costly, high turnover.

Psychologically speaking, a defensive reaction is also the unconscious inner-child lashing out. The unconscious is the part of the mind that has primal needs that were not met when we were kids, which is behind a lot of our reactions as adults. In pop-psychology terms, it is called pushing our buttons. Even if you came from a home that looked like a Norman Rockwell painting, you have pain points. We all have them. It is just part of being a human being.

When I sat with myself and thought about why my first

reaction to my employee was bitter defensiveness, I realized that I was upset because I had never asked for "me time." In 30 years of working 60 to 100 hours a week, on weekends, over the holidays and during vacations, I do not recall ever seriously thinking that I could completely detach from work during any of it.

I am certain that my then-husband, Brian, suggested I find more work-life balance while we were married, but I am equally certain that I never gave it a passing thought. I may have even laughed at him or scolded him for suggesting it. Familiar retorts to Brian when we were having the all-too-common fight about me being a workaholic included:

"I have to work these hours; I am the head of the department."

"I have to work these hours; I want to move up the corporate ladder."

"I have to work these hours, because my female boss—the president of the company—works these hours."

There was a saying in corporate America, which I was taught while working at my first job at a Los Angeles PR agency: "If you do not show up for work on Saturday, don't bother coming in on Sunday, because you're fired."

The defensive reaction that Boomers and Gen Xers have to Millennial employees is about us: our upbringing, our belief systems, and the inner child in our unconscious. Basically, it is about a lot of things that have nothing to with what our Millennial employees are asking for. Therefore, I do not believe the word entitled is a fair descriptor for Millennials. I see Millennial behavior in the workplace differently.

I believe that Millennials have a distinctive worldview that sets them apart from prior generations. A lot of Gen Xers and Baby Boomers saw the excesses of the 1980s and rebelled. They subsequently raised their children to believe that every life is sacred (some of us admittedly got that from *Monty Python: The Meaning of Life*). They also taught their kids that all people are created equal, and that everyone is a winner (remember the years when everyone got a trophy on sports teams).

Those teachings are manifesting for Millennials in several different ways:

1   **Millennials believe in work-life balance.**
2   **They are good at setting boundaries around their needs.**
3   **They have the confidence that they can, and should, win at the game of life.**

Imagine this scenario: A Millennial employee sets a strong boundary with his boss that he needs to leave at a certain time every day to go to a yoga class. His exercise regime is an important practice that helps him think and perform better on the job. Or perhaps a Millennial employee schedules a vacation to go on a meditation retreat and refuses to respond to emails while she is gone, so that she can get away from the office, rejuvenate and get some perspective.

When you take into account the values with which Millennials were raised, you can see how those teachings shaped their psychology. Millennials highly value their humanness. This understanding comes from the positive lessons they were taught by their parents, vis-a-vis work-life balance, strong boundaries and believing they can win at anything they try.

Therefore, Boomer and Gen X colleagues often say Millennials are entitled and lazy. In fact, entitlement is a word that is as interconnected to the American Millennial as peanut butter is to jelly. But I do not think that they are entitled, so I am offering a theory, which I will posit in the form of a question.

Are Millennials really entitled, or do they have a completely different way of valuing the human experience? Many Millennials view humanness in a way that older generations do not, which is part of what is causing the divide between the younger and older generations in corporate America.

So far, entitled is not a moniker shared by Gen Z. I suspect that parents saw what the "everybody gets a trophy" practice was doing in reality and stopped. It did not take long to realize that they were inadvertently raising a generation of people who would have a hard time dealing with life's inevitable disappointments if they thought they should always win at everything.

Next, You're Going to Tell Me That They're Really Team Players

Another character trait that frequently gets eye rolls from older generations is Millennials as team players. Millennials are known for being collaborative and team oriented.[6] This does not mean they are team players, as Boomers and Gen X would define the term.

A 2013 study released by EY, formerly Ernst & Young, looked at the differences between Baby Boomers, Gen X and Millennials in the workplace.[7] The study found that Millennials ranked high when it came to them being enthusiastic about their jobs, with 68 percent of respondents agreeing with that statement. However, they ranked lower as team players (45 percent of those surveyed agreed) and hard-working (only 39 percent agreed).

Well, there is a difference in business between being a team player—which means to do whatever it takes to get the job done, regardless of your title, position or stated job responsibilities—and being teamwork oriented, which means working better when collaborating in a group than working on one's own.

The idea that Millennials are not team players is reinforced by the perception that they are entitled. Meanwhile, Millennials are classic collaborators. They like being in groups. Think of their style as a college study session. Everyone is around a table or in a living room-esque setup of comfy chairs with headphones on, typing away at their computers. One person looks up and asks a question of the others, they all give their opinion, and then the group goes back to working quietly… together.

I have been at several companies that have completely redesigned their headquarters to accommodate the teamwork orientation of these younger employees. Open workspaces have taken over as innumerable companies follow the Silicon Valley tech giants to create a more collaborative workplace with fewer offices, more social gathering areas, and conference rooms for group work. The spaces encourage younger workers to roam freely with their laptops and cell phones, since technological advances mean that they no longer need to be tethered to a desk.

The design change was positive for Millennials, since it fosters workplace well-being, something that Millennials and other generations identify as being more important than material benefits. However, it proved challenging for Gen Xers and Baby Boomers, who are used to the privacy and quiet of an office.

As with many trends, the much-maligned open workspace may be short lived. Instituted by tech companies and embraced by Hollywood, innumerable startups, coworking spaces like WeWork and Regus, and now even banks, the open workspace may not be as positive an experience for Gen Zers, who are independent and seem to like to work on their own. I am sure the Boomers and Gen Xers will not mind rearranging the workspace again to accommo- date more offices. I do not know a single colleague who happily embraced losing his or her office to work in a highly distracting bullpen where you cannot concentrate or even hear yourself think.

A Virtual Army of Young Adults in the United States

Before we go further, I want to take a moment to put all of the generations in context, because you will find differing opin- ions on the age ranges of all of them. As an expert on younger generations, I use the Pew Research Center as one of the prima- ry authorities in defining generational timespans, due to Pew's mission and its stellar reputation for conducting data-driven social science research.

Millennials are generally thought of as having been born between 1981 and 1996,[8] while members of the Gen Z cohort are believed to have been born between 1997 and 2010.[9] Roughly speaking, employees and consumers who are 39 and younger as of 2020 are part of these two generational cohorts. This means that Gen Z started entering the workplace in and around 2015.

Pew has not identified the final birth year for Gen Z yet. However, Mark McCrindle, a generational researcher in Australia and noted TEDx speaker, espouses that anyone born in 2010 or later is part of what is initially being labeled as Generation Alpha.[10] There is a brief chapter on Gen Alpha at the end of this book. I say brief because the oldest of them are currently nine years old, so we are

just getting to know them and how they will impact our world…
but that did not stop me from asking them what they think!

For context, Millennials were preceded by Gen X, born
1965–1980; Baby Boomers, born 1946–1964; the Silent Generation,
born 1928-1945; and the GI Generation, born before 1928.[11] It is
interesting to note that the older generations—Boomers, Silent and
GI—all span 18, 19 and 24 years, respectively, while Gen X and
Millennials span 16 years and Gen Z looks like it could span just
14 years.

G.I. Generation born before 1928
The Silent Generation born 1928–1945
Baby Boomers born 1946–1964
Gen X born 1965–1980
Millennials born 1981–1996
Gen Z born 1997–2010*
Generation Alpha born 2010–present

(*As mentioned, 2010 and Generation Alpha are not yet acknowledged by Pew.)

My working hypothesis for the shortening timespan of the
various generations is that the word "generation" is defined as "a
group of individuals born and living contemporaneously."[12] The
nicknames we give different generations are to help marketers
identify the psychographic similarities that result from people
being born, raised and influenced by the era in which they are living. The psychographics include parallels in personality, opinions,
attitudes, interests and lifestyles.

As modern society has progressed, the pace of change has
quickened. In the early 1900s, industrial and technological change
was slower than it is today, which meant that access to information was not as prevalent and people were more isolated in their
communities and belief systems. As technology has progressed,
societal changes occur more rapidly, which in turn leads to a more
rapid change in opinions, attitudes and interests. Ergo, the timespan we use to identify people of different generations is shortening.

Since different authorities use varying dates to define the
generations, it is challenging to get a definitive count on their size.

While it is safe to say that Millennials and Generation Z comprise an army, the actual number depends on what years are being used to describe the two generations.

Millennials are currently the largest generation in the work-force,[13] while Gen Z is the largest generation in the United States, surpassing the Baby Boomers.[14] Pew estimates that there are 71 million Millennials in the United States,[15] which was nearly 22 percent of the U.S. population in 2019.[16] Millennials are between the ages of 24- and 39-years old in 2020, so there are more of them in the workforce, but Gen Z is coming.

The oldest Gen Zers are 23 years old and have only recently entered the workforce. At their youngest, they are 10 years old as of 2020. In total, Gen Z is estimated to be 27 percent of the American population,[17] which means there were 88.8 million of them as of May 2019.[18]

The two generations are also the most diverse populations in the United States, with Millennials surpassing any generation before them and Gen Z surpassing Millennials. A study conducted by Merrill Lynch in October 2018, stated that Millennials are 56 percent white and 44 percent other ethnicities, while Gen Z is 50 percent white and 50 percent other ethnicities.[19]

Now that we have defined the years, let us look at these two generations—the events that shaped them and the attitudes, opinions, lifestyles and interests they have. There are differences, but there are a lot of similarities that speak to why they are having such a big impact on American society.

What's in a Name? And Does the Proverbial Shoe Fit?

As Shakespeare wrote in *Romeo and Juliet*, "What's in a name? That which we call a rose by any other name would smell as sweet."[20] Well, sweet or not, like many recent generations, Millennials do not like their generational nickname, because they do not think of themselves as a homogenous group.[21]

Millennials were first called Gen Y back when they were just kids born in the early 1980s. Then 2000 happened—we partied like it was 1999, the 20th century became the 21st century, and over-night the young adults entering the workforce stopped being Gen Y and became known as Millennials. As marketers tried to identify this generation to better sell them products, it became clear that this group did not want to be identified as a uniform package to which you could mass market.

The Millennials were right. There are a lot of differences within any generation, so labeling them is always an exercise in assigning descriptions in broad terms. Of course, all generations have the shared experience of being brought up during the same era, which causes certain unavoidable similarities. So, despite their efforts not to be stereotyped, there are stereotypes that apply.

The fact that Millennials collectively bristle at being called Millennials and reject any traits assigned to them is, in and of itself, a character trait. Frankly, Gen X felt the same way about themselves, which is one of the reasons why they were termed Gen X, as in generation unknowable. This is the same use of "X" that is seen in innumerable pop culture references, especially TV series, such as the *X-Factor* and *X-Files*. It connotes the unknowable quality or trait that everyone strives to have.

> **NOTE:** The X-Files *was so popular in the mid-1990s that a series of companion guides were published, which sold very well. The first official companion guide—written in 1995 by my future ex-husband Brian Lowry—was titled,* The Truth Is Out There. *The implication of the series was that the truth was unknowable.*

But let us get back to the topic of hating the character traits and name assigned to your generation, because Gen Z also hates their name. I think very few people in America want to be typecast as one thing or another. (Although, Hollywood has been typecasting actors since the advent of the movies and it seems to work for them.)

Gen Z was initially nicknamed iGen because they have never known a world that is not digitally connected thanks to the iPhone and other smartphones that followed it. In 2018, the *New York Times* conducted a poll on social media and asked their young readers what they think about the name Gen Z.[22] The *Times* received thousands of replies.

According to the *Times*, the most popular post in their Facebook poll came from Alexandra Della Santina, 22, in Philadelphia, who suggested that Gen Z be renamed Generation Scapegoat, since older generations are going to need a new "punching bag" after they are done criticizing Millennials. The second most popular post in the Facebook poll came from Kiernan Majerus-Collins, 22, in Maine, who stated: "Don't call us anything. The whole notion of cohesive generations is nonsense."

Finally, on the name iGen, one respondent in the *New York Times* research expressed her support of the name Gen Z and her rebuff of the term iGen quite cogently. Raquel Glassner, 22, of Washington, said in the article, "I've never heard iGeneration before, but that is really horrendous. Our whole generation shouldn't be branded by Apple. Gen Z is the final generation of the 1900s, and a generational title using the last letter in the alphabet seems fitting."

The Significant Moments for Two Generations of Americans

Historic events define and shape each generation. The economy, international relations, domestic politics and the rapid growth of technology all set the stage for some of the key defining moments for Millennials and Gen Z.

Born in 1981, the oldest of Millennials were just 20 years old when the United States experienced a large-scale, terrorist attack unlike anything in modern history on September 11, 2001.

A few years later, Facebook launched in February 2004 (at first only available to Millennial college students), charting the path for the explosion of social media and the complete loss of privacy, and—some would say—decency. It paved the way for YouTube (2005), Twitter (2006), WhatsApp (2009), Instagram (2010) and Snapchat (2011).

Millennials started on Facebook, but many subsequently moved to Instagram when Facebook became too commercial and too old—Gen X and the Baby Boomers migrated to the platform to check up on their kids and grandkids but stayed for the social connections with long-lost friends. By the time Gen Z was old enough to use social media, they skipped Facebook and Twitter all together and gravitated to Instagram and Snapchat—a confusing technology that repels older adults, who cannot intuitively understand it. Gen Zers and younger Millennials are also currently flocking to TikTok, with 1.5 billion downloads of the app worldwide as of December 2019.[23]

Another historic event for both generations was the Great Recession from December 2007 to June 2009, which triggered a financial struggle that had a detrimental effect on Millennial earnings and savings. The majority of Millennials were trying to enter the workforce just before or during the Great Recession and, as a result, they currently do not have enough money to retire at 65.[24]

Gen Z was too young to be financially independent during that recession, but they watched their parents and older siblings struggle through it. They also dealt with the changes that come when families have to downsize their lifestyles during a major economic downturn, such as the one the United States experienced in 2008.

In the midst of the Recession, we elected the first African American president, Barack Obama, on November 4, 2008. Voters ages 18 to 30 overwhelmingly preferred Obama by 66 percent.[25] At the time, the oldest Millennials were 27 and their generation made up the majority of young adult voters.

Eight years later, the U.S. saw the election of Donald Trump over Hillary Clinton, a shocking turn of events because polling had suggested that Clinton would win the election. Whether you support Trump or oppose him, he has become a divisive and polarizing figure in the United States, which has led members of Gen Z to take to social media to express themselves on a variety of issues.

Since Trump took office, America has gotten a good look at how iGen uses social media as a bully pulpit to express themselves, lead a purpose-driven life and effect change in our country. More than previous generations, Millennials and Gen Z place a high value on serving a purpose in life and having a job in which they contribute meaningfully to the world.

The reason for that is obvious when you take a look at Gen Z's parents, who are primarily members of Generation X (born 1965–1980). Gen X is a small generation labeled the "latchkey kids," a term coined in the early 1900s, but popularized in the 1980s to describe this generation, which came home from school to an empty house or lived without a lot of parental supervision, because the majority of parents both worked.[26]

Innumerable articles written about Gen X call them the "lost generation," because of their small size and jaded attitude toward life (many grew up in the wake of Watergate and the Vietnam War, during the height of the Cold War with Russia). The rock band Nirvana is frequently cited as having written the anthem for this generation.

Not surprisingly, as parents, Gen X is trying to give their kids the safe, idyllic childhood they would have wanted, but did not have. They do it by being present and showing up for their children in a way that their own parents could not.[27]

Generation Z has come of age in the best economy the United States has ever had. At their oldest, they were teenagers when the Great Recession hit. They watched their parents deal with the repercussions of the worst economy most Americans have ever experienced. As a result, they do not trust corporate America or Wall Street, but their pain points—the defining moments that have shaped them—are not singular incidents, such as the attacks on U.S. soil on 9/11, or the election of the country's first African American president in 2008. Gen Z's stressors come from ongoing problems happening daily in the U.S., which are deeply rooted in the fabric of our country and the foundation of our society.

A research report issued by the American Psychological Association (APA) in 2018 found that 75 percent of Gen Z respondents said that mass shootings are a major source of stress, while 72 percent of them say that school shootings are a source of stress.[28] In addition, 58 percent of the Gen Z respondents worry about global warming and climate change and 53 percent worry about sexual harassment and assault.

Most generations can point to specific incidents—both bad and good—that shocked them and shaped their worldview. Gen Z's worldview was formed by watching in fear what happens around them daily.

Like the Hippie movement of the 1960s, Gen Z has a distinct moral compass that separates them from older generations like the Baby Boomers and Gen X. In a *New York Times* article in 2019, writer David Brooks characterized Gen Z as having "a sense of vocation, moral call, and a rage at injustice that is a legitimate rejection of what came before."[29]

It is important to remind ourselves here that Gen Z is the first all-digital generation. These are the kids who were taking selfies and effortlessly flipping through YouTube videos at two years old. Because of their early fluency on smartphones and tablets, they were exposed to news and events at a younger age than any generation before them. Therefore, it is not surprising that their stress comes from pervasive topics in the news.

The Boomerang Generations

During this master class on Millennials and Gen Z, it is vital to look at how their financial situation is impacting their personal and professional lives. Human capital is the most important asset on the balance sheet. The key to your organization's success is understanding its young adult employees, consumers and investors, so you can better serve them.

The problem for young adults, especially Millennials, is that they have more debt than previous generations. In early 2019, the New York Federal Reserve Consumer Credit Panel reported that Americans between the ages of 19 and 29 were carrying over $1 trillion in debt for the first time ever.[30] This debt included student loans, credit cards and mortgages.

Meanwhile, starting salaries have not gone up, but prices have.[31] Economists say that the U.S. is in a period of economic growth and inflation is low, but many Americans feel squeezed, especially Millennials and Gen Z. Prices are rising. Wages are not. Obviously, that is a problem for the lower and middle classes.

It makes sense that young adults have more debt than ever. Younger employees and consumers have less time in the workforce, so they have fewer investments and savings to pay off that debt than older generations. Meanwhile, they are being squeezed by a higher cost of living and shrinking wages. Seems like Economics 101 to me, and yet Wall Street, the politicians and the media constantly tout the great economy and health and well-being of the American people. That sounds like we are living in an episode of *The Twilight Zone*.

According to a 2019 published study from Merrill Lynch Wealth Management, 70 percent of Americans between the ages of 18 and 34 relied on financial support from their parents in the past year. To put a solid number on that statistic, parents in the U.S. are spending a total of $500 billion dollars a year helping their Millennial and Gen Z kids make it in today's economy.[32]

The same Merrill Lynch Wealth Management study shares that "Early adults are much more likely to describe the life stage as a roller coaster (30 percent), a juggling act (24 percent) or climbing a mountain (24 percent) than a day at the beach (8 percent)."[33]

Dependence on their parents has created an interesting phenomenon. Young adult children between the ages of 18 and 35 are returning home in higher numbers than ever before, because they cannot afford to be financially independent. The media have dubbed the trend the Boomerang Generation. Multiple generations of families living together is a tradition that exists in other cultures, such as China, India and Japan, but it has not been the norm in the United States in the modern era.

The good news is that according to the Merrill Lynch study, 79 percent of the so-called boomerangs say that they like living at home with their parents and 87 percent of the parents say they like having their adult children at home.[34]

The Middle of the Country vs. the Coasts

This chapter is about looking at the known psychographic

traits of two large and powerful generations in the United States and helping you understand who they are, why they are that way and how you can better work with them... assuming you are not a Millennial or Gen Zer. However, it is important to note that psychographics, which are attitudes, opinions, lifestyles and interests, provide broad guidelines, but do not apply to everyone in the generation. We need to be mindful that generations have similarities because they grow up in the same era and have shared experiences of those times, but they are still unique individuals.

Not surprisingly for those who live in the United States, there are major differences in the personalities of Americans who live on the East and West Coasts and those who live in the middle of the country, which comprises the Southwest, Midwest and Southeast. The stark social, political and economic regional differences in the United States are part of why it is difficult to paint any U.S. generation with a broad brush.

In 2015, New Heartland Group commissioned a study from Prince Market Research to study Millennials in what they call the "new heartland."[35] They found that there are significant differences between them and coastal Millennials. They are a very diverse group, racially and ethnically, but the study says they share "core values like faith, community and family."[36]

Compared to their coastal counterparts, new heartland Millennials marry earlier and have children sooner, which leads them to buy homes and make other household and life decisions earlier. Conversely, Millennials on either coast focus on finding a good job and getting professional degrees. Their time horizon for marriage is in the ensuing 10 years, so nearly a decade on average after Millennials living in the middle of the country.

The study also measured certain psychographics and found that 54 percent of the new heartland Millennials identified faith as a core value versus 38 percent of the coastal Millennials. While 51 percent of the coastal Millennials identified social responsibility as a core value, 44 percent of the heartland Millennials said they valued it.[37]

While the study focused on Millennials, the differences that it highlights are reflected in all generations—from Gen Z and Gen X to Boomers and Silents. Generational differences explain a lot about people's beliefs and work habits, but geography in a country as large as the United States is also a factor.

Sex, Drugs and Rock & Roll? Not If You're a Gen Zer!

I want to spend a few pages focused on Gen Z. As a generation, they are not yet as well-known as Millennials, which makes sense. Gen Z entered the labor force en masse less than five years ago. Meanwhile, Millennials are older, so more has been written about them.

If Millennials were the catalyst for socially conscious generations, Gen Z is the sober generation.[38] Literally and figuratively, this is a group that delayed drinking, sex and driving (not necessarily in that order). Raised primarily by Generation X, Gen Z had helicopter parents, who created a secure relationship with an open line of dialogue and an atmosphere of safety. This means that rites of passage—like drinking alcohol, having sex and driving—could wait. Uber also helped, since going out with friends as teenagers did not mean having to drive.

So, who is Gen Z? Again, there is no single way to describe an entire generation, but in aggregate, this is a group of Americans who spend more time on social media than any other generation.[39] I can tell you from my experience of getting brand messages to Gen Z on social media that they prefer Snapchat and are not on Facebook, since Facebook is now inhabited by their Gen X parents, as well as their Baby Boomer and Silent Generation grandparents.

As a result of their digital proclivity, they have more access to information than any generation before them. Interestingly, one result of that access is that they are very brand conscious, which we see daily in the number of young adults who take to social media to call for boycotts of companies and institutions that do things with which they disagree.

Gen Zers are also very conscious of money. Members of Generation Z were young children during the Great Recession of 2008, so they watched their parents get laid off and families struggle financially.

While Millennials tend to be oriented toward teamwork, Gen Z is more individualistic and competitive.[40] Parents and schools had reversed the "everybody gets a trophy" idea when they realized they were raising a group of humans that struggled to deal with loss and disappointment. A quick about-face occurred, and parents began teaching their Generation Z progeny to have pride in their work as individuals and to play to win but lose graciously and move on quickly from failure. Google's famous pillar of innovation—"fail fast"—is the rally cry to think outside the box, go for it and then get out quickly if it is not working.

In my experience of working with Gen Z employees, they are diligent, eager to please and constantly need to be learning new things. I believe this is because the moms and dads raising Generation Z did not grow up in a purely digital era, so they recognize the importance of developing skills in order to get ahead and stay relevant, which they have instilled in their Gen Z children.

To that point, Gen X passed on a key lesson they were taught—you have to work for your success. Despite the fact that the U.S. is in a booming economy, there has been a decline in financial solvency from generation to generation.[41] The Silent Generation did very well for itself and the Baby Boomers took the ball and ran with it.[42] Gen X got slammed by multiple recessions, which started as the oldest of them were coming out of college, and Millennials got TKO'd by the Great Recession in 2008.[43]

Gen Z is not immune to this financial issue, despite the good economy. In 2016, the Pew Research Center issued a study about finances for young adults ages 18 to 34. The study stated that 32.1 percent of young adults live in their parents' home, while 22 percent lived with another family member or non-relative. When the study looked at diverse racial groups, it found that record numbers of African American and Hispanic young adults (36 percent each) lived in their parents' house.[44]

Gen Z is determined to do it differently and have been taught by their parents that success is not a birthright. Interestingly, this teaching may be leading to fewer of them pursuing higher education. In 2014, a Business Insider article stated that 64 percent of Gen Zers were considering college, as opposed to 71 percent of Millennials.[45]

It did not take universities long to figure out that trend. In 2019, I was asked to teach a graduate-level course at Columbia on corporate communications. As I prepared the syllabus, I looked at a plethora of books and business case studies that would engage my students in theoretical discussions about crisis communications and product publicity based on real-world situations, just as I had been taught in college.

Nope! I was told by the head of the department at Columbia that I had to make the learning practical, as if the class was being taught in a trade school. She informed me that today's students— both Millennials and Gen Z—want to be given practical skills that they can bring into the workforce. If they are not learning skills that can immediately translate into their work life, they are not engaged.

This shift in education, from an emphasis in studying liberal arts to obtaining degrees with practical application in the workforce, makes sense when you also consider that Gen Z is more entrepreneurial than Millennials.[46] After all, being an entrepreneur is simpler than ever. It is not easy, but it is simple. Technology enables anybody to start a business and social media enables them to market and promote it quickly and cheaply.

In addition, entrepreneurs have had extreme success in the digital age with ideas that solve a problem in the marketplace. Think: Airbnb, Lyft, Snapchat, Spotify and 23andMe, just to name a few.

Which brings me to another point: the financial rewards can be tremendous. All of the companies named above are unicorns—a startup that is valued at over $1 billion BEFORE it goes public. In other words, the genius entrepreneurs who came up with these innovative ideas are extremely rich even before the initial public offering (IPO).

It is important to note that Gen Z is motivated by financial security, but not at the expense of their values. This generation cares about making a difference in the world. In order to feel fulfilled, they need to feel like they are contributing in some meaningful way. This could be a reason why so many of them are interested in being entrepreneurs.[47]

A final word on a key Gen Z personality trait that has found its way to Millennials, as well as their Generation X parents: Personalization is their mantra—they want what they want when they want it. They live in an on-demand world created not by them, but by the tech companies, media conglomerates and online retailers that have allowed them to get anything they want at the click of a button. Whether it is Amazon, Apple, Netflix, Snapchat, Spotify, Uber or Venmo, young people live in a world of near instant gratification.

CHAPTER 2 | YOU RAISED THEM, NOW YOU HAVE TO LIVE WITH THEM IN THE WORKPLACE

"You raised them, now you have to live with them in the workplace" was the original title for this book. When my Gen X, Baby Boomer and Silent Generation friends and colleagues complain about the changes that Millennials and Gen Z are bringing to the workplace, politics and society as a whole, I like to remind them that we raised them and now we have to adjust to the changes that come with them. We instilled Millennials and Gen Z with important values and now we are seeing the effects of it at work. We were happy to teach them to value themselves and have balance in their lives, but we did not like it when they brought those ideas into our workplace.

Why is that? We need to look at the unique attitudes, opinions, lifestyles and interests of these three older generations, because we have five generations together in the workforce for the first time in history. With workers as young as 18 and as old as 85, the differences in opinions, attitudes and life experiences are causing a massive amount of misunderstandings and conflict.

Silent Generation Statistics and Psychographics

Remembering that generational birth years are approximations, Pew Research states that the Silent Generation was born between 1928 and 1945 and is thus named because they grew up during the Great Depression and World War II. As a result, their proclivity is to comply with societal rules and be politically aware and involved.[48] It is also possible that the name came from the McCarthy era, during which anyone suspected of being a communist sympathizer could be brought before a government panel, lose their job and be put in prison. This made it dangerous for people to speak about their beliefs outside of the home.

On rare occasions, I see this generation referred to as the Traditionalists. I suspect it is because of their formal ways and old-fashioned morals. Pew does not use this generational moniker for Silents, so I will not either, but I mention it in case you have heard a different name for this group.

Overall, the Silent Generation grew up in a period of extreme hardship. During the Great Depression people lost their jobs, their homes and many were starving. The Dust Bowl—a drought in the Southern region in the 1930s—compounded the impact of the Depression, as crops failed, and farm families migrated west.[49]

As a result of this difficult period, Silents are a relatively small generation with just 47 million members at their height.[50] That is several million people less than Generation X (55 million), which is also known for being a small and relatively quiet generation.[51]

This is a racially homogenous generation. The Silent Generation comprises 78 percent Non-Hispanic White, 8 percent Hispanic, 8 percent African American, 4 percent Asian and 1 percent other ethnicities.[52]

In looking at their lifestyles, 64 percent of the Silent Generation were married between the ages of 18 and 33 years old.[53] That is relatively young compared to when Millennials are getting married today.

Religion is another area where we see homogeny, with 85 percent of the Silent Generation identifying as members of a Christian denomination, four percent as "other groups" and only 11 percent saying they do not identify with any religion.[54]

In terms of politics, the Silents lean Republican, so they

expound conservative social values that run counter to the more Democratic-leaning Millennials.[55] Pew Research conducted a Political Polarization survey in 2014 and found that 39 percent of Silents expressed consistently conservative or mostly conservative views. While this is not a majority, it is significantly more than Baby Boomers at 33 percent, Gen X at 25 percent and Millennials at 15 percent.[56]

As of 2020, the youngest of these elder statesmen are 75 and some can still be found in the workforce. Examples include Joe Biden, former Vice President of the United States and candidate for U.S. president in 2020, who was born in 1942. Since I am talking about politicians, Senator Bernie Sanders, a candidate for U.S. president in 2016 and in 2020, was born in 1941. In fact, as of 2019, 23 of the 100 U.S. Senators were born in 1945 or earlier.[57]

People are living longer and working longer, which is why we have five generations together in the workplace, whether it is in private business or government. Several Fortune 500 CEOs are members of the Silent Generation, including Warren Buffett of Berkshire Hathaway, born 1930; Sheldon Adelson of The Las Vegas Sands, born 1930; Roger Penske of Penske Automotive Group, born 1937; Leslie Wexner of L Brands, also born 1937; and Alan Miller of Universal Health Services, born 1937.[58]

Baby Boomer Statistics and Psychographics

With 76 million members, Baby Boomers (born 1946-1964) were the largest generation in American history, until Gen Z came along.[59] The reason is because they were born in the era that began at the end of World War II and culminated in the early 1960s when the birth control pill became widely available.[60]

Baby Boomers were the Hippies—breaking societal norms for everything from the music they listened to and how they dressed to the books they read and the drugs they took. Boomers were rebellious; they pushed boundaries and staged peaceful demonstrations fighting for the rights that seemed obvious to them.

If that sounds familiar, it should. There are uncanny sim-

ilarities between the defiance and societal shifts caused by the
Boomers in the 1960s and 70s and the major awakening American society is undergoing today. Like the Boomers, Gen Z and
Millennials are railing against issues they see as crushing their
generations. They use the power of social media to amplify their
thoughts about everything from climate change and gun control to
issues surrounding equality and immigration.

Unlike these younger generations, Boomers are not a diverse
population, although researchers can see the percentages growing as compared to the Silent Generation. Non-Hispanic White
comprises 72 percent of Boomers (versus 78 percent for Silents),
while 11 percent of Boomers are African American, 10 percent are
Hispanic, 5 percent are Asian, and 2 percent are other ethnicities.[61]

In terms of their lifestyle choices, 49 percent of Baby Boomers were married between the ages of 18 and 33, which is significantly less than Silents, but more than Gen X and Millennials.

Not surprisingly, the religious beliefs of Baby Boomers are
closely affiliated with the Silent Generation, although the trend is
toward less identification as members of a Christian denomination
(78 percent for Boomers versus 85 percent for Silents) and more
toward other beliefs or unaffiliated (22 percent for Boomers versus
15 percent for the Silents).[62]

The political leanings of Baby Boomers are not as clear cut
as they are with Silents. Members of this generation who came
into voting age during Nixon's presidency are more Democratic
than younger Boomers, who started voting during the Carter and
Reagan eras.[63] Boomers tend to go along with social changes more
than Silents, but they are still more conservative than the younger
generations.[64] Despite their Hippie roots, Boomers are more traditional than younger generations and tend to believe that marriage
is between a man and a woman and same-sex couples should not
raise children.[65]

Baby Boomers are creating a lot of the logjam in the workplace today, because they are staying in the workforce longer than
any generation before them. Pew research states that 29 percent of
those Baby Boomers who have passed the traditional retirement

age of 65 years old were working or looking for work in 2018.[66] This is not surprising, given that Boomers do not think old age starts until you reach your seventies.[67]

Generation X Statistics and Psychographics

Born between 1965 and 1980, Gen X is one of the smallest generations in the United States with only 55 million members, which earned them the nickname of the Baby Bust.[68] As mentioned earlier, they have also been called the latchkey kids because they grew up in households where both parents worked and they came home from school to an empty house. Infinitely nicknamable, Gen X was also later dubbed America's middle child—the "overlooked generation" sandwiched between two huge generations with the Baby Boomers before them and Millennials after them.[69]

Researchers and the media have not paid a lot of attention to this smaller generation, instead turning their attention to the larger and louder Baby Boomers and Millennials. Why? Because Gen X is literally the perfect middle child—not as financially secure as the Boomers, but better off than the Millennials;[70] not as politically or socially conservative as the Boomers, but not as liberal as the Millennials; more technologically oriented than the Boomers, but not as tech savvy as Millennials.[71] And on and on it goes.

In keeping with the middle child theme, Gen X is more racially diverse than the Boomers, but not as much as Millennials. With Gen X, there was a significant decline in the percentage of people identifying as Non-Hispanic White (61 percent of Gen X versus 72 percent of Boomers), while Hispanic (18 percent), African American (12 percent) and Asian (7 percent) all increased versus Boomers and Silents.[72]

Given the era in which Gen Xers were raised, it is not surprising that the trend toward marrying later in life continued. Only 38 percent of Gen Xers married between the ages of 18 and 33, compared with 49 percent of Boomers and 64 percent of Silents.[73]

Religious identity is another area where Pew researchers see a continuous trend. Only 70 percent of Gen Xers identify as Christian as do just 56 percent of Millennials.[74] The percentages of those identifying as other religions or unaffiliated grew correspondingly.

Like Baby Boomers, Gen X is a generation divided when it comes to politics. Older Gen Xers came into voting age during Reagan's second term and they lean Republican.[75] Reaganomics benefited older Gen Xers entering the workforce and the country saw the end of the cold war. Younger Gen Xers started voting at the end of Bush Sr.'s tumultuous one-term presidency and the start of Clinton's eight-year run, and lean Democrat.[76]

The More Things Change, the More They Stay the Same

The generational divide is nothing new. As the popular 1980s song says, "Every generation blames the one before." British rock band Mike and the Mechanics wrote those lyrics in their 1988 hit "The Living Years," and the song does a good job of encapsulating what we see with every generation.

As teenagers and twentysomethings, we think the prior generations messed up the world and that our generation has to fix it. We often have a lot of proof that says we are right about this. Look at the Boomers and the Hippie counterculture movement protesting the world created by the Silent and G.I Generations. Look at Gen Z taking on climate change and gun violence.

When we are older, we often do not understand the younger generations. We think that age and experience will give them the perspective they need to "grow out of" the idealistic phase and become more pragmatic about the world and how it works.

With every generation, we see massive changes that the older generations push back against—from clothing and music to changes in language and lifestyle. At some point in your life, you have probably heard your parents, grandparents, or a boss say, "You know, in my day, we did things differently." The not-so-subtle implication being that life was better back then.

You say you just don't see it
He says it's perfect sense
You just can't get agreement
In this present tense
We all talk a different language
Talking in defense

Lyrics from "The Living Years"

The changes we are seeing today in society and in the workplace seem dramatic, but they are also to be expected. We have two massive generations—Millennials and Gen Z—making their way through life. My goal with this book is to explain what is happening and why it is happening in a way that is relatable and accessible, so that we can all better understand each other.

I believe that when we understand where someone else is coming from, why they think the way they do, or why they see something in a different way, we are more tolerant of what they need, and our reactions are not as defensive. This makes it easier to get along at work and in life. There is less name calling and more problem solving.

I will repeat this a few times in this book, but intolerance met with intolerance just leads to more intolerance. Or, as Mike and the Mechanics said, "We all talk a different language talking in defense."

CHAPTER 3 | THE CULTURAL ZEITGEIST OF GILLENNIALS

The title is not a typo. In the world of mashups, Gen Z and Millennial together is shorter as Gillennial. We will see if it sticks.

As we know, Gen Z is the first fully digital generation. They have never known a world without cell phones and the internet. The iPhone did not come along until the older ones were around 10 years old, but the youngest Gen Zers were instinctively tapping on smartphones and swiping away to get to the next screen by the age of two.

Millennials were born in an analog era, but the internet gained wide-spread consumer use in the mid-1990s, while they were still in high school. They came of age at a time when a vast amount of information was available on computer. No more pulling out the encyclopedia after asking mom and dad a question over dinner that they could not answer.

Thanks to social media, these two generations are more connected to friends, families, colleagues and total strangers than any of the generations that have come before them. In business, older generations value picking up the phone or having a face-to-face meeting. But American Millennials and Gen Z workers consider digital communications to be faster and more effective—unless they are being ghosted (not responded to). In that case, I have seen young adult staffers resort to the old-fashioned way... after being urged by an older boss, like me, who knows that they can get answers through a phone call.

I considered it a huge victory for older generations when one of my Millennial staffers, who had been stressing over not being able to reach a reporter for days, finally followed my suggestion and called the reporter on the phone. Miraculously, she got the answer she needed after the reporter actually answered his phone.

In fairness, it is possible that the reporter was so stunned that the telephone on his desk was ringing that he may have picked it up as a novelty. We cannot know the answer to that, but either way, making an old-fashioned phone call worked!

However, technology is both a blessing and a curse for these two generations. They are more connected than ever, but they use social media to gauge their personal, professional and financial status in life. I call it Digital Compare-and-Despair Syndrome. Younger people do not have the life perspective to understand that what they are seeing is just one side of the story.

Digital Compare-and-Despair Syndrome

On social media, people post about their joy and success, and share their loss and sorrow. But there is a line that people rarely cross on social media—I know that is hard to believe. With very few exceptions, your friends and family rarely share the ugly side of life in the moment.

Think about it for a minute.

An acquaintance on social media always posts pictures while out drinking at concerts and glamorous parties. You assume she has an incredible life with a lot of friends. You compare your life to hers and despair. Why is she always out socializing while you are at home alone? A few months later, you notice that your same acquaintance is posting more pictures than usual of her dog, her hike in the mountains and funny comments about celebrities. It is a subtle shift and her life still looks good to you. However, what happened behind the scenes, which she never posts on her socials, is that all of the fun was masking a problem with alcohol—she got fired from her job and she is making new friends while getting help for her drinking problem.

Your other friend posts a beautiful video of his engagement after he asks his girlfriend of just six months to marry him. You assume they are happy, and you are jealous—why does he get to find love and get married quickly, while you have one unsuccessful date after another? You later find out that his fiancée has anger control issues and is emotionally and physically abusing him. He could not admit to himself or to anyone else that he was being abused by a woman. He finally broke off the engagement, but never posted about the trials and tribulations on socials. It was too mortifying.

A friend who is beautiful, successful and happily married constantly posts darling pictures of her children with all their achievements and their adorable pets doing cute things. What she never says to anyone, except maybe her therapist, is that despite the blessings in her life, her internal voice sounds like an abusive parent, and it constantly tells her, "You are fat, ugly and a failure." While you are looking at her social media life through rose colored glasses, this horrifying mantra causes her to see life in depressing shades of gray and she is contemplating suicide.

In a study about young adults (identified as being between the ages of 18 and 34), nearly half of them (49 percent) admit to "feeling addicted to social media," and 68 percent have "fear of missing out on what they see their peers doing."[77]

A lot has been written about FOMO—fear of missing out—and the very real depression and anxiety that it creates. It primarily impacts young adults from 18 to 33 years old and causes feelings of insecurity and low social status that are triggered by viewing the social media posts of friends and acquaintances.[78]

Research released in March 2019 found that suicide and mood disorders, including depression and anxiety, have increased among teens and young adults, who are identified in the study as being age 18 to 25.[79] Depression went up from 8.1 percent in 2005 to 13.2 percent in 2017; thoughts of suicide, attempts, and actual deaths increased from 7 percent in 2009 to 10.3 percent in 2017. The study did not specifically measure for why the U.S. is seeing an increase, but the researchers state that other studies have shown that people who spend more time surfing social media are more likely to feel depressed and unhappy.

Culture and the younger generations appear to be fighting back against the idyllic portrayal of life as depicted on social media. When Instagram first started, i.e., before it had 1 billion monthly users, Millennials and Gen Z gravitated to it for the picture-perfect shot. For social media influencers of all ages (mostly in their teens and twenties) that meant a heavily planned and edited photo, similar to what you would see in a magazine spread, except shot on an iPhone with filters instead of with a million dollars of equipment, location fees and stylists.

The perfect-photo fad drove the popularity of photo-filter apps with digital effects that provided ideal lighting and smooth skin to make everyone look like a movie star. This phenomenon only played into the insecurities and anxieties of the rest of the social media world, as young adults—mostly girls—compared and despaired while trying to keep up with the Kardashians (literally and figuratively).

But like any fad that becomes overdone, younger members of Generation Z, who are in their early teens, reject the overly manufactured, perfectly on-brand photo style for a messier-than-life, raw look that has catapulted them to the head of the next influencer craze. By mid-2019, *The Atlantic* was proclaiming that perfect is out, while real and raw are in, and today's influencers are doctoring the photos to make themselves and the images look worse.[80]

For those of us with perspective, i.e., old people who have been around for a few more decades than the rest, the dramatic shift is not a surprise. History repeats itself and fads constantly swing back and forth like the metal balls of the addicting swinging pendulum toy, Newton's Cradle.

If you think about it, what is happening on Instagram is not any different than what happened in the early days of television.

Perfectly dressed housewives with their perfect families paraded around prime-time TV in the 1950s. *I Love Lucy* (1951) and *Ozzie and Harriet* (1952) ruled the airwaves until the social climate changed and sitcoms chased the trends to feature single working women in *The Mary Tyler Moore Show* (1970) and *Laverne & Shirley* (1976), along with divorced bachelors in *The Odd Couple* (1970).

The shift in the TV landscape took a few decades, while the shift in the digital era on Instagram only took a few years, but it is hard to ignore the similarities. Cultural trends swing dramatically when popularity becomes oversaturated, and culturally accepted practices historically swing 180 degrees in the opposite direction.

I am stating the obvious, but it is worth saying: Happy people are more productive people. If your workers are depressed (and remember that Millennials are the largest generation in the workforce today), those unhappy workers will not function at their best when they are at work. If worker productivity is down, then your revenues go down. If workers are unhappy, their unhappiness translates to your customers and clients—and, again, revenues suffer. If workers are distracted by personal problems, your business risk goes up, because human beings make mistakes when they are upset, distracted or fearful.

In 2019, while I was working as a consultant, I developed an employee sentiment survey for clients to use to "take the temperature" of their organizations, because studies have shown that employees prefer workplace well-being to material benefits.[81] A positive working environment can contribute to workplace well-being, but organizations have a vested interest in providing benefits and perks that help their employees maintain positive mental health.

Their Purpose Is to Live a Life of Purpose

Millennials and Generation Z have a strong focus on doing social good.[82] Their parents instilled them with important lessons about human rights, equality, the environment and faith. These issues are essential to them as consumers, employees and investors. However, an important side note here is that many of their interests do not focus as much on feel-good philanthropy, which is characterized as more self-indulgent than helpful.

Professor Peter Singer at Princeton University penned an opinion piece in the *Washington Post* that makes a logical argument against contributing to Make-A-Wish, where the average wish cost $7,500 in 2013 (when the piece was published).[83] Professor Singer argued that your donation money would positively impact more lives if spent on a charity that provides bed nets to regions with malaria outbreaks or to a charity that helps solve food shortages in Malawi.

Millennials and Gen Z were educated in an era when schools and parents emphasized equality, respect for others and the environment, and volunteer work in order to get into college, so both generations are largely dedicated to living a life of purpose. This translates to a basic human trait—we all share this one—the more interested we are, the more engaged we are.[84] But with Millennials and Gen Z, their interest is in fairness and equality, as much as it is in earning a living.

This is why the "gig economy" is in and corporate America is out on their list of what is lit and what is not lit (for those of you who are over 50 years old, "lit" means cool).

Not surprisingly, these two generations care about sustainable investing, also referred to as socially responsible investing, which comprises feel-good investments with generally lower returns. For those high net worth and ultra-high net worth Millennials and Gen Zers, it is part of their portfolios.[85]

As mentioned earlier, Millennials and Gen Z are the most digitally connected generations in the U.S., which means that they are jointly more connected to news and information than any other generations. So, it is not a surprise that they have a hyper-awareness of the world around them.

The environment is a growing issue for Millennials and Gen Z. In a Harvard Institute of Politics (IOP) poll, 46 percent of young adults (ages 18 to 29) believe the government should be doing more to prevent or slow climate change.[86] That is up 14 percentage points from 2015 when Harvard polled young adults with the same question.

The Harvard IOP poll also found that young adults in the U.S. are increasingly "concerned about the moral direction of the country"—61 percent agreed with that statement in 2019 while 52 percent agreed in the 2015 poll.[87]

On topics that generally divide conservatives and liberals, Gen Z is more open. There are certain life choices that are natural to them and not political. For example, in a recent Pew Research poll that examined political leanings of young adults, 59 percent of Gen Zers think online profiles should allow people to identify as something other than a man or a woman.[88] An example of this could be Gender Nonconforming, Gender Diverse or Transgender Female/Transgender Male. This is compared to 50 percent of Millennials and 40 percent or less of Gen Xers, Baby Boomers and the Silent Generation.

Given this, it is not surprising that personal preferences for using gender-neutral pronouns has grown. In the same study, a little over one third (35 percent) of Gen Zers know someone who does not identify as either he/him/his or she/her/hers, but as the gender-neutral equivalent, which in English is they/them/theirs. This is compared to 25 percent of Millennials, who know someone who identifies by gender-neutral pronouns.

Since Gen Z is the most racially diverse generational cohort in American history, it is not surprising that 62 percent of them think racial diversity is a good thing.[89] This is in line with the 61 percent of Millennials who say the same.

Same-sex marriage is still an area that is divided. Less than half of Gen Zers (48 percent) and Millennials (47 percent) believe that gays and lesbians should be allowed to legally marry.[90] However, when asked if they think same-sex marriage has a bad effect on society, only 15 percent of Gen Zers and Millennials said it was bad.

Companies are learning to pay attention to young adults and their focus on social good, purpose and mission-driven values. It is important to young adults—and Gen Z in particular—that the companies they work for, and buy from as consumers, are aligned with their social values. These values can be conservative or liberal, but they want to know what your company stands for and your actions need to match that purpose.

For example, NFL quarterback Colin Kaepernick, a Millennial, made a provocative statement in 2016 by taking a knee during the singing of the National Anthem at football games to protest police treatment of minorities. After two years of NFL players kneeling during the National Anthem and an intense controversy over freedom of speech versus respect for the American flag, Nike featured Kaepernick in one of its "Just Do It" ads, clearly signaling its support for racial equality and justice. Moreover, it spoke directly to Nike's stated mission, which is "'To bring inspiration and innovation to every athlete* in the world.' *If you have a body, you are an athlete."[91]

Similarly, Chick-fil-A is a chain of fast food restaurants headquartered in Atlanta. The company expounds Christian values in its mission statement and in practice. It is even closed on Sundays. On the company's corporate website, it states that its corporate purpose is "To glorify God by being a faithful steward of all that is entrusted to us and to have a positive influence on all who come into contact with Chick-fil-A."[92]

They clearly state and support their purpose by donating millions of dollars to charities that share their Christian values, including the Salvation Army and the Fellowship of Christian Athletes.[93] While both Nike and Chick-fil-A take a lot of criticism from people who oppose their corporate stance, they also gain support and brand loyalty from consumers, especially young adults, who agree with their positions.

This is new for corporate America. Prior to social media, companies were blank slates. The prevailing wisdom was that you needed to be everything for everybody to attract the most customers. Whether the business was a fast food chain, an athletic apparel company, a movie studio, a computer manufacturer or a Big Four accounting firm, they did not stand for anything, because they stood to serve everybody.

Social media changed all of that. While MySpace and LinkedIn gained popularity in the early 2000s, social media did not hit its stride until Facebook (2004) and YouTube (2005) came onto the scene. As companies embraced social media as a way to market to the masses, they also entered an uncomfortable new reality in which they had to let go of controlling the message and allow fans—and foes—to engage with them on social platforms.

This practice was met with skepticism and caution at first. Debates raged inside corporate America about who should control the social channels—the PR or marketing department. If PR oversaw the company's social media postings, the social channels were a steady drumbeat of well planned, highly controlled, and admittedly boring messages. I can say that because I was one of those in-house communications executives carefully controlling brand reputation management on Twitter and fighting with my various heads of marketing over it. If marketing controlled the channels, the messages were a barrage of splashy, hard-sell ads to buy, buy, buy.

What changed? One pivotal moment was the blackout during the 2013 Super Bowl at the Superdome in New Orleans. CBS was broadcasting the game, which was in the 3rd quarter, when the power went out and caused the game to come to a screeching and seemingly endless halt. The lights eventually went back on, but not until after one fast-acting brand had made news by coming out with the Tweet of the day. Oreo posted the following, which was retweeted 10,000 times in an hour: "Power out? No problem. You can still dunk in the dark."[94]

Why did Oreo make waves that day? Because companies did not do that type of thing back then. You needed corporate sign off on everything you said and did on social media, just like you did for any advertisement, marketing mailer or press release.

By Oreo's own admission, the reason they were able to act so quickly was because the corporate marketing leads and their digital agency were all sitting together during the game to monitor social sentiment of their ads. In other words, that tweet still went through the usual approval process, but it happened within minutes thanks to the fact that all of the key decision makers were in the same room during the Super Bowl.[95]

Today, many social media managers are empowered to speak in the voice of the brand and are given the autonomy to respond quickly to customers and situations, because Millennials and Gen Z expect it. Remember, these young adults are an on-demand group, who want what they want when they want it and where they want it. They expect the companies they consume and work for to be the same.

Why Advertisers Covet Them, and Why You Should Too

In the United States, our society embraces youth and youth culture. Advertisers pay more money to reach younger consumers than older ones for two reasons.

First, it is important to get products in front of people at an early age, while we are establishing habits that will become ingrained in us in our forties and fifties. Why are habits a thing? Because people resist change.

Second, it is harder to reach younger people. The reasons are anthropological and societal. In America today, a lot of people are getting married and starting families later. Therefore, more twenty- and thirty-somethings are single, unencumbered by family obligations and more likely to be out at night. As a result, Americans in their twenties and into their thirties have less time to watch content on TV or online, play video games, and read newspapers and magazines (usually online). These are all primary ways that advertisers reach consumers with their messages.

Conversely, people in their forties, fifties and beyond have time to consume more content in traditional ways—watching TV, reading a newspaper or magazine (either online or in print) and looking up medical ailments on the internet. Americans in their forties and fifties may have family obligations at home in the evening, kids and jobs to tend to early in the morning and, of course, our bodies change, so we have less energy to do the things we used to do in our twenties—hence the expression, youth is wasted on the young.

Older adults, aged 55 and above, are easier for advertisers

to reach, since they tend to have more time to consume the types of media where advertisers place their ads. As a result, the advertisers pay less to advertise to them. Advertising is about supply and demand. You pay more for the thing that is in short supply. It is harder to get your ads in front of young adults, which makes reaching them more valuable; therefore, the ads cost more.

In college, I became very socially conscious thanks to some political science classes. After a few classes in politics and civics, I began to think I knew more than the adults. As an 18-year-old, I did not have a lot of opportunity to express or act on my ideas, because there was no such thing as YouTube, Instagram, Reddit or even the internet. That is probably a blessing. I shudder to think what I would have posted on social media during high school and college.

As an adult, I came to realize that my 18-year-old self and my friends were shaping consumer purchasing and the future of business. Advertising has always reflected the likes and dislikes of younger audiences. Since its inception, it has been a youth-driven industry that is primarily focused on appearance and the pursuit of an ideal. That ideal changes with time. In the late 1970s, it was the beautiful, independent woman, who could "bring home the bacon, fry it up in a pan" (thank you, Enjoli perfume). In 2019, that ideal was the highly controversial Gillette ad, "We Believe: The Best Men Can Be," which told guys to stop being brutes and start showing up in life as woke men.

In the United States, youth culture drives a lot of the innovation and change we experience. As businesses react to the personalities and trends of the next generation, we all experience a seismic shift in the way we operate. According to *Forbes*, Gen Z has $143 billion in spending power and advertisers are salivating.[96] In 2020, this generation spans ages 10 to 23 years old, so they are forming buying habits. This is an open road for advertisers, and it is why they are chomping at the bit to get ads in front of these kids.

Meanwhile, Millennial spending power as of 2020 is projected to be $1.5 trillion.[97] That puts the combined spending power of

Gen Z and Millennials at more than $1.6 trillion. It is also important to note that Gen Z affects an additional $1.2 trillion in spending, when you factor in the influence they have on spending by their parents.[98]

If only Netflix, Hulu and Amazon would quit ruining the plan by providing commercial-free streaming programming! Do they not know that television shows were made to bring eyeballs to advertising?! ... And you thought the point of TV was so you could be entertained. Wrong! It is so advertisers can show their commercials.

That may be a jaded statement, but it is also somewhat true. Have you ever wondered why new TV series premiere in September? It goes back to the advent of black-and-white TV. September is when automobile companies introduce their new car lines for the coming year, and they made the TV networks provide original programming at that time of year, so more people would see the ads for their cars.

Same goes for magazines. They exist for the full-page, glossy print ads. Without the ads, there are no magazines. Without people reading magazines, there are no ads. This is why the print editions of your favorite newspapers and magazines are razor thin today. No one reads the print editions anymore, so there are very few ads, so the publishers have ceased many print publications. It is also why you cannot go online without 10 ads popping up and dancing around to get your attention. Everyone gets their news digitally these days.

They Don't Go to the News, Because the News Comes to Them

Since I work in public relations, my job is to figure out where 18-to-34-year-olds are getting their information, so I can make sure my companies are covered in those outlets. In the early 2000s, I realized that young adults were not getting their news from traditional media outlets.

I used to run communications for UPN, which was one of

six broadcast TV networks. Every morning, an assistant in my department came in very early and pulled newspaper, magazine and TV news clips that mentioned our programs. She compiled all of them in a report and printed it to circulate to our executives.

There could be over 100 stories each day and it was the early 2000s, so we did not yet distribute the clip report digitally. Executives were still in the habit of having them printed out and hand delivered by my assistant. In September and January, when we typically premiered new TV series, the daily clip report would be two-to-three-inches thick.

Newspapers around the country and national magazine outlets used to write tons of articles about our shows, but the number of people who watched our programming was tiny compared to our competitors at the other networks, including ABC, CBS, NBC and Fox. Frankly, MTV would occasionally beat us in the Nielsen ratings! (Nielsen ratings are a system of measurement used by the television industry to determine how many people watch any given TV show and its commercials.)

How could we have this much press coverage and no 18-to-34-year-olds watching our TV series?!

It did not take a rocket scientist to figure out that we had two issues. The first has to do with how the TV ratings system works. It tries, but it does not adequately measure young adult viewing.

Second, young people were not watching because they did not know about our shows. The reason they did not know about our shows was because young adults were not reading the *Los Angeles Times*, *USA Today*, and *Entertainment Weekly* the way they used to, and they were no longer watching shows like *Entertainment Tonight* and *The View*.

That was nearly 20 years ago, when the majority of Americans still got their news from a printed newspaper that was delivered to their doorstep every morning, or from TV news. It was also before social media.

Today, young adults do not go looking for news; news goes looking for them. What do I mean by that? The best way to explain it is by regaling you with a conversation I recently had with a financial advisor I will call "John," who is under the age of 30.

To set the stage, this advisor works at a Wall Street investment firm, has high net worth clients, has been in his profession for nine years and attended an Ivy League college. He is Caucasian and he was wearing a suit and bowtie when I met him. By all outward appearances, this is someone who reads the *Wall Street Journal* (WSJ) and has CNBC playing in the background at home and at work.

I was at an event in New York City when I met John, who was standing with an older gentleman in his seventies. We started to talk about what we each do for a living and I told the two of them that I am an expert in communicating with Millennials and Gen Z as employees and consumers. This kicked off our conversation about the character traits of these two generations.

When I talk about Millennials and Gen Z, I like to illustrate what I am saying with stories. I told them one of my favorite anecdotes about the challenges that blue-chip companies face today when they try to communicate important corporate messages to younger investors.

In December of 2018, Reuters wrote a very damaging article about Johnson & Johnson (J&J), which cited an internal memo from the 1970s, among other sources, that indicated the company knew there were traces of asbestos in its talcum powder.[99] J&J immediately went into full damage control by putting its CEO Alex Gorsky on CNBC's "Mad Money" and taking out full-page ads in the *New York Times* (NYT) and the *Wall Street Journal*. They also issued a statement from the company to major media outlets, which they posted on their own website and social channels.

As a crisis PR specialist, I can confirm that everything J&J's PR team did was a flawlessly executed, textbook response to the situation... if the textbook had been written in the 1980s.

J&J definitely reached older investors by going to the WSJ, NYT and CNBC. However, they did not get their message to many investors under the age of 35—nor did they get it to the moms who are using J&J's baby talcum powder on their infants. The reason is because plenty of media outlets where young adults get their news ran follow-up stories about the Reuters article. None of them ran J&J's response.

It appears as though J&J did not target its response to digitally native press. Now, that could have been intentional. There are plenty of times in a communications crisis when I have tried to mitigate the blowback by responding, but not broadcasting the response. However, if you want to talk to anyone under the age of 35, you have to go outside of traditional media outlets.

After I finished telling the J&J story, John (remember, he works on Wall Street) volunteered for us that he does not read the *Journal* or the *Times*. Shocked, the gentleman in his seventies apprehensively asked John where he goes to get his news.

John casually replied, "I don't go anywhere to get my news. News comes to me."

I sat there nodding my head knowingly. You see, young adults do not get news in the traditional way. They get news through aggregator websites and platforms, such as the Drudge Report, the Apple News widget on the iPhone and social media platforms, such as Snapchat and Twitter.

Social media algorithms are programmed to serve up information that is relevant to you. That means, they send you what is familiar from sources that you visit frequently. Since a lot of this information includes news posted by various sources, including friends and family, people believe they are well informed. It is true that we have more information than ever before. However, a lot of that information is highly curated and caters to our specific tastes and preferences.

John continued, "And, if I happen to miss something, well, if the news is big enough, it eventually finds me."

You will find that statement shocking if you fall into one or more of these categories: (1) you are over the age of 60, (2) you work at a company that does not cater to young adults, so you do not have experience with their habits, and/or (3) you work in the news media and have fooled yourself into believing young adults still consume news the old fashioned way—one magazine or newspaper at a time.

Is Snapchat the Only Way to Reach Them?

Millennials and Gen Z young adults are a highly coveted, hard-to-reach demographic. Below is what you need to know about how to reach them… for now. It will change in a heartbeat and the best way to stay on top of trends is to employ a lot of young adult workers, listen to their ideas, and then give them the autonomy to innovate and the authority to enact change, because the bottom line is that your bottom line depends on it. These two generations are changing the corporate world at such a rapid pace that organizations that do not ride the wave of change will end up getting clobbered by it.

1   Celebrity endorsements do not work on young adults as well as they used to, because the message is not genuine, since the celebrity is paid exorbitant amounts of money to promote a product or service.[100]

2   Digital media influencers—both macro (100,000+ followers) and mega (1 million+ followers)—have little influence with these two generations for the same reason that celebrities have no influence.

3   Micro influencers were hot and now they are not. Average Joes or Janes with fewer than 50,000 followers on social media were thought to be more believable, because they were not being paid by marketers… but now they are (being paid), so they are not (believable). Got it? Good!

So, how do these young adults get recommendations, find out about new products, decide what to buy and what not to buy? Most rely on word-of-mouth (WOM) from family members, friends and significant others. An *AdWeek* article indicated that 89 percent of young adults trust these sources more than the brands themselves.[101]

A key thing to remember with Gen Z in particular is that they grew up honing their own brand on social media. This means that we now have an entire generation of branding experts, and they are discerning customers, so reviews are important. Once they get a recommendation, 93 percent read the reviews before making their decision, according to *AdWeek*.

By the way, WOM marketing does not just apply to products and services; this is also the way Millennials and Gen Z make investments and decide where they want to work. As employees, consumers and investors, young adults are immune to and even skeptical of corporate messaging.

The best way to reach them is through family and friends and the way to do that is by being everywhere that they are. That means being on every screen they use—from the smartphone and tablet to the TV and laptop. These multitasking maniacs often juggle Snapchat, YouTube and Netflix, all while shopping online.

While older Millennials still like to look online, but buy in person, Gen Z has entered *The Jetsons* era. It is as much about time as it is about convenience. Why would they take the time to go out to shop when they can do it from their phone while commuting to and from work or school? Brick-and-mortar shopping is not in vogue, but retailers are working hard to attract young consumers and it is possible they could stage a comeback.

Now that you know *the who* and *the where* of marketing to Millennials and Gen Z, let us talk about *the how*.

The best line I have heard about *how* to create brand messages for Gen Z came from a *Forbes* article. It said, "Don't create ads—create value."[102]

The way to message young adults, and especially Gen Z, is by making it worth their time to watch or read your message. Gen Z and younger Millennials grew up with the ability to quickly and easily filter messages. If they do not like what they are seeing or reading, they just move to the next instant-gratification platform that will give them what they want when they want it. Remember, these are the on-demand generations.

Yes, it is about what is in it for them. It is also about how you can help them make a difference in the world. The bygone era of day dreamers is over and the days of doing it are here. The technology that lives in the palm of our hands gives young adults the power to change the world and they are changing it—not planning on changing it, they are actually changing it.

I was on the Board of Directors of an international nonprofit called The Resolution Project. We provide funding and mentorship to college-aged entrepreneurs who have businesses that do social good. These Millennials, and now Gen Zers, are not waiting for the grownups to teach them how to be entrepreneurs and business leaders, they are going out and doing it and then checking in and saying, "I have this cool idea that I have already implemented on a small scale, but I could use a few resources. Do you think you could give me a hand, so I can save the world that you messed up? Please and thank you!"

> **A side note:** *I love Gen Z. They are changing the world and instead of being skeptical and scared, I look at it as my job to help older generations and companies embrace the change that Gen Z is bringing, because it is happening whether we like it or not.*

Whether you want them to buy your product or service, to come work for your company, or to invest in your business, your message is competing with an overly saturated content marketplace for the attention of people who get their entertainment in 6-second spurts (think TikTok and Vine) or 140 characters (okay, Twitter upped it to 280, but you get the idea). You have to grab their attention fast with the perfect Instagram photo, the eye-catching video thumbnail on YouTube, or the scintillating headline as they scroll through the Discover section of their Snapchat feed.

Ultimately, the best way to engage Millennial and Gen Z consumers with your brand message is by being authentic yourself. Whether you are marketing a product, selling a service, recruiting an employee or pitching an investor, these young adults want to work for and buy from companies that are aligned with their social values.

CHAPTER 4 | DEALING WITH OUR DIFFERENCES

As with all generations, Millennials and Gen Z have different views of the world than their predecessors. They are breaking conventional norms, up leveling social values and changing how we do business. This is nothing new. This is what a new generation does, and it is how society progresses. However, these two generations are having a more radical effect than we have seen in decades, and it is causing a lot of friction in the business world.

As parents, teachers and mentors, we instilled these two generations with different values, and then we developed the technologies that now act as a megaphone for their opinions and experiences on social media. In fact, thanks to social media, Millennials and Gen Z are forcing change in the public and private sectors with a speed and intensity that no previous generations could.

Americans working in Fortune 500 companies who are in their fifties, sixties and seventies have a different work style and ethic than workers in their twenties and thirties. The older executives in the U.S. came into the workplace and blindly followed previous generations into a workaholic mindset thinking that they had to pay their dues and work long hours to get ahead. Thanks to the Blackberry and now smartphones, executives in their sixties and seventies are still working 24/7/365. So, when do they actually get to enjoy life and not be workaholics?

Meanwhile, workers in their twenties and thirties have said a big, fat "No, thank you" to that practice. Younger workers raised in a different era with different philosophies and world events than older workers are turning down jobs at Fortune 500 companies in exchange for freelance work, more autonomy and work-life balance. This is causing a big problem for corporations looking to recruit and retain the best young talent.

Is it then a surprise that the generations that came before—Gen X, Baby Boomers and the Silent Generation—are defensive and resistant to the ideas and attitudes of these younger people?

No! It is not a surprise. In fact, it could be predicted.

Regardless, it is causing a struggle in business that is likened to a game of tug-o-war in grammar school.

Older Generations: "We have to do it my way!"

Younger Generations: "I don't want to and I'm not going to."

Older Generations: "No! My way."

Younger Generations: "Actually, I don't need to do it your way. You see, there are startup companies that will give me more flexibility to have work-life balance AND there is this thing called the gig economy, where I don't have to be a servant in corporate America. In fact, I am happier and more fulfilled when I have my own business or work as a freelancer.

"And there is this thing called social media, where I can market my ideas and services. In fact, I have so many opportunities to create my own thing on my own terms, I am going to be an entrepreneur.

"So, you can keep your paltry salary with its tiny 2 percent annual increase and your subpar benefits package. I don't think it's fair and, more importantly, I don't need it."

A version of this conversation is being carried out daily in companies across the United States. A 50-year spread in the ages of everyone in the workforce today means there are a ton of differences in attitudes, opinions, lifestyles, and experience. Senior managers (i.e., older workers) tend to be practical and adhere to old conventions, while ignoring the cultural nuances entering the workplace with these new generations. The result is that it is regularly costing senior people their jobs and costing companies a lot of money in lawsuits and damaged brand reputations.

I have a radical position on this, which my Gen X peers and our Baby Boomer colleagues are also coming to realize. Millennials and Gen Z are not going to adapt to us. We need to adapt to them. We do not have a choice, because these two generations have a lot of choices.

Benjamin Franklin famously said that there are only two things that are certain in life—death and taxes.

Well, I would argue that the one thing death and taxes have in common is that they both create a change in your life. So, in my personal philosophy, the one guarantee in life is change. Change is inevitable and it is unavoidable. Yet many human beings instinctively resist change.

I was taught by my bosses Dawn Ostroff, whom I worked for at UPN, The CW and Condé Nast, and Nancy Tellem at CBS to embrace change, reject the status quo and take risks on implementing new ideas. While working for both Dawn and Nancy, I saw some executives resist the changes that these two visionaries were bringing, but we cannot know if something new is going to work unless we try it. They taught me that you either get on at the front of the train and drive it or jump on the caboose and get dragged.

The media industry is on the forefront of every technological change that happens in society. Content drives consumption. The entertainment industry produces and distributes content. Therefore, TV, film, magazines and digital video makers are forced to change as innovation and technology shift.

I also ascribe to the philosophy that you should fail fast. If something you are experimenting with does not work, get out fast. Tantamount to this philosophy is that you have to be willing to fail, because if you do not, it means you are not innovating and growing with the one thing that is inevitable in life—change!

Change or die. That is the lesson of evolution of the human

species and it is the lesson facing corporate America today. The way to embrace change is to (1) acknowledge that it is happening, (2) educate yourself about what is happening and (3) work with your team to find the solutions that best fit your needs.

Five Generations in the Workforce

For the first time ever, we have five generations in the workforce, which makes being at work like attending a dysfunctional-family Thanksgiving dinner every single day of the week. If you are chuckling uncomfortably right now, then you have experienced what I am talking about.

Navigating the psycho-social differences between five generations in today's office environment is challenging. In order to artfully navigate it, we need to understand where each generation is coming from and their work styles. A challenging workplace negatively impacts worker productivity, increases business risk, hurts brand reputation and affects your ability to recruit and retain good employees. The bottom line is your organization's bottom line, so this is about real dollars and sense (yes, the alternative spelling is intended).

The Silent Generation at Work

Remember that this is the generation that lived through the Great Depression with 24 percent unemployment rate[103] and Americans starving to death, as well as World War II. When they were growing up, life was tough and resources were scarce. As a result, having a job is a privilege and they work very hard.[104] Their belief is that you climb your way to the top through hard work, long hours and solid performance.[105] There are no shortcuts or quick fixes.

Another aspect of this generation's work ethic is best summarized by my mother. Whenever she or I are met with adversity, she says, "Like a workhorse, you just put your blinders on and keep moving straight ahead." The Silents grew up in extremely difficult conditions, so they know that doggedness and stick-toitiveness are what you need to eventually succeed.

A few other character traits of employees from the Silent Generation include that they are loyal—many of them stay with the same organization for their entire careers; respect authority; are frugal with budgets and company resources; and have old-fashioned morals, so they are safe and consistent. They can also be tech challenged. For most of them, computers and smartphones are not as intuitive as they are for younger generations.[106]

Many of these traits are in stark contrast to younger workers, who expect opportunities at work before they have put in the time and proven themselves, and who do not pledge allegiance to any company, because they know corporate America will not be loyal to them. Remember, older Millennials could not find jobs when they got out of college during the Great Recession and Gen Z watched their parents lose their jobs and not be able to find work during that period.

Baby Boomers at Work

Everything I am about to tell you about Baby Boomers will not surprise you. I think that a lot of the generational information is instinctive and intuitive when we hear it, primarily because we have parents, grandparents and other family members who model it for us.

Baby Boomers are all about work. They are the original workaholics, but they are in it for the glamour and the glory, not the joy of it. I know a lot of them will bristle at that. It is an overgeneralization, but if you ask a Boomer who they are, they will tell you what they do for a living.[107] A C-suite title, a corner office and the perks that come with their lofty positions are what motivate a Boomer.

Because Boomers were the Hippies, the ones who set out to change the world, they have spent decades in the workforce believing they can change the business world, too. Some of their prominent character traits at work include being independent, goal driven, team oriented, disciplined and competitive.[108]

Boomers also believe in equal opportunity. That is not surprising, given that they protested for women's rights and were the first generation to see an influx of women entering the American workforce. Like the Silents, Boomers believe that hard work and a proven track record means they should sit in the corner office. Some Boomers struggle with technology, but many have adapted.

Most importantly, like the Silent Generation, Boomers lean toward hierarchical structure and discipline.[109] This obviously creates problems in traditional companies where Boomers are in charge and resist the new ideas and demands of Millennials and Gen Z workers.

Gen X at Work

Gen X, a.k.a. America's middle child, followed the Boomers into the workforce like lemmings and emulated their work ethic and habits. Like good middle children, Gen X did not ask questions or make waves. They kept the peace by doing as they were told.

Also, in keeping with their middle child moniker, Gen Xers are good at making friends and are agreeable. The mantra of Gen X in the workforce should be, "Can we all just get along, people?" The flip side to being agreeable is that Gen X is not likely to speak up if they disagree with a manager or a boss.[110] Certainly, they are less likely to do so than Millennials and Gen Z.

Gen X is appreciated by their Silent and Boomer bosses, because they are among the best workers in the labor force today. They are flexible, independent, technologically inclined, hardworking and like to have fun.[111] They value work-life balance, but they do not have much of it—at least none that I have personally experienced for myself or with my peers!

Since Gen Xers are more flexible, they are adapting better to the changes being brought about in the workplace by Millennials and Gen Z. In typical middle child fashion, they serve as a bridge in your organization between young staffers and senior managers. Gen X is also more likely to switch jobs after three to five years, so they relate with the younger generations, who believe you have to constantly move around in order to get ahead in your career.

Millennials at Work

Millennials are the largest generation in the workforce today, so at this point in their career trajectory, we are seeing the full force of the changes they expect. Hopefully, the first two chapters of this book helped debunk some of the stereotypes about Millennials, so we can instead view them as a generation brought up with good boundaries and healthy ideas about work-life balance. Therefore, flexibility at work is important to them, so they can pursue personal interests. Whether it is attending a yoga retreat or leaving early to take music lessons, they learned from their workaholic Baby Boomer and Gen X parents that work-life balance is necessary—think of it as one of those life lessons that falls under, "Do as I say, not as I do."

Millennials are the most educated generation in the country—more of them went to college than any generation before them. They are technologically savvy, occupy jobs for skilled workers and expect to move up the executive ranks quickly. This can cause problems for managers from older generations, who think employees need to "do the grunt work" and "pay their dues" before getting access to the glamorous projects and face time with the clients or C-suite executives. (If you are not familiar with that term, it is shorthand for the top positions in a corporation that have the word "chief" in the title, such as Chief Executive Officer, Chief Financial Officer and Chief Operating Officer.)

The oldest Millennials entered the workforce at the start of the Great Recession, but for the ensuing 10 years, the United States experienced an unprecedented period of economic growth. Therefore, Millennials job hop—a lot! Many will leave a company after just 18 to 24 months for a 10 percent salary increase and an interesting perk. This is a very expensive problem for companies, since it costs approximately 1.5 times an employee's salary to replace them.

It is likely that the speed with which Millennials switch jobs will slow down during an economic correction or recession. Regardless, it is ingrained in them to move jobs a lot. It used to be that Gen X and Baby Boomer managers would look at a resume and, if the applicant moved around every two or three years, they assumed there was something wrong with that person's performance. Today, Millennials believe that if they stay at a job for longer than two years, it means there is something wrong with their performance, because they cannot get a bigger, better job somewhere else. This whole notion is bonkers to the Silents, who believed you should work at one company for your entire career.

The biggest problem with Millennials moving around a lot is that it negatively impacts a company's bottom line, since the company has to continually recruit and retain new workers. Millennials will stay in a job if there are clear opportunities for growth and they believe they are being groomed to be executives and move up the corporate ladder quickly.

You may have noticed that Millennials are looking for more feedback on their job performance than companies are used to giving. Millennials received a lot of input from teachers and parents. Constant communication was the theme of their childhood. So, this is a generation that wants frequent input on their performance. They also like working in groups. The feedback loop of group work is fun and motivating for Millennials. I mentioned this in the first chapter. They are not team players, in the colloquial use of the term, but they like working in teams.

Finally, one of the biggest changes we are seeing as a result of having Millennials in the workforce is that we raised them to be aware of social issues, which they brought with them into the workforce. Millennials and Gen Z both expect the companies they work for to have clearly stated values that are reinforced by how the company conducts itself with its customers, employees and as corporate citizens. This is not something that companies used to do. Corporations preferred to stay neutral and not take a stance on social issues, so they could be everything to everybody. After all, you might not eat my chocolate bar, drink my soda or wear my sneakers if I say or do something that runs counter to your political beliefs.

Gen Z at Work

Welcome to a world with iGen in the workforce—they are

technologically astute, well-educated and independent. As of 2020, the oldest members of Gen Z are 23 years old, so we have not yet experienced everything that this massive generation has to offer, but we are getting a good idea of what they expect. Remember, Gen Z is the largest generation in the U.S., surpassing the Baby Boomers in size, so once they are fully in the workforce, the changes will be enormous.

Gen Z has more power at their fingertips than any generation before them and they know how to use it—unlike the Gen Xers, Boomers and Silents. This makes Gen Z a force to be reckoned with. They are a highly entrepreneurial generation, which is not surprising. They have grown up in an era where a smartphone, Wi-Fi connection and innovative idea are all you need to start a business. As a result, they switch jobs quickly and often, with a twist. These workers will leave their corporate job after just a few months in order to launch their own company or go to work for a friend's startup.

Like Millennials, Gen Zers in the workforce are highly educated, occupy professional jobs, expect to work on interesting projects, have access to management, and move up the corporate ladder quickly. They, too, want constant feedback on their job performance.

Gen Z is also values oriented and issues driven. More than Millennials, Gen Z insists that the companies they work for and buy from share their values. Also, transparency is key. After all, they are used to having all of the answers to their questions at their fingertips. So, it is not surprising that they also expect their employers to provide information, be open and forthcoming.

While Millennials are known for idealism, Gen Z is known for its pragmatic approach to life. This is a generation that is more socially aware than any generation before them, but there is a catch. Later in the book, I examine whether or not they are forcing a shift that is making us too politically correct. There is a nuanced line between "no tolerance" policies and allowing people to be human, make mistakes and learn from them.

Many say that the U.S. was overdue for an up leveling in

our behavior toward women and other disenfranchised minorities, but some corporate policies have jumped the shark on political correctness, making it impossible for anyone to say anything out of fear of being fired or ostracized. (Those of you who remember *Happy Days* will appreciate that throwback reference, which was coined after a ridiculously goofy episode in which the star character Fonzie jumps a shark on water skis… while wearing his signature leather jacket.)

The problem with the morality police is that, as we tighten our grip on what is allowed and not allowed, eventually everyone except a small minority will get caught on the wrong side of that judgement.

I do not want to sound like a broken record, but it is important to reiterate that generational experts and marketers make sweeping generalities about large groups of people—especially the largest generation in the United States, which is Generation Z. There are exceptions to every rule. There are people who fit the paradigm and those who do not. Not every Silent, Boomer, Gen Xer, Millennial or Gen Zer fits into every category in this book. The point is that these are broad characterizations that can be applied to the many, but not all.

Dealing with our Differences: How to Play Nice in the Corporate Sandbox

With five generations in the workforce, miscommunications and misunderstandings will happen—frequently! We are talking about people as young as 18 and people as old as their 80s, who were raised in very different eras, with different rules and different socially acceptable behaviors. We do not all see life the same. In fact, it is impossible for us to do so, and those differences are what makes a company successful.

Gen Z and Millennials embrace individuality and differences. The older generations can learn from them.

With the help of time and experience, older generations have learned tolerance and understanding. Gen Zers and Millennials can learn from them.

We cannot solve for the generational differences in business—or in life. What companies can do is educate their employees about the differences. As human beings, we have the capacity for understanding. Through understanding, we learn. Through learning, we change.

While there are many psychological theories about how to influence people, one of the most popular theories about it came from businessman Dale Carnegie, who wrote the famous book, *How to Win Friends and Influence People*.[112] Carnegie outlined 30 principles for how to handle people, get them to like you, win them over to your way of thinking, and help change them. I will highlight a few below.

1   "If You Want to Gather Honey, Don't Kick Over the Beehive."[113] In his first principle, Carnegie says not to criticize people, shame them or condemn them. This is based on the English proverb: You catch more flies with honey than with vinegar.

2   Carnegie's "The Big Secret of Dealing with People"[114] is to be curious about people. Ask questions and be sincerely interested in what someone says. Carnegie liked this principle so much that he included this idea in his list three different times. Each time, the bottom line is to be a good listener and encourage others to talk about themselves—a lot.

     I would add that when you listen, consider where that person is coming from. For example, if you are talking to an older worker from the Silent Generation, consider that they grew up during the Depression and, when they were kids, they had to carefully unwrap their birthday gifts so they could reuse the wrapping paper and boxes, because there was a shortage of materials, as well as money to buy them. Maybe they are a Gen Xer, brought up during the excess of the 1980s when they tore open gifts and threw the wrapping paper and boxes away in big plastic garbage bags. Or maybe they are a Gen Zer, who has existential angst about using paper and boxes because of the harm it does to the environment.

3 "You Can't Win an Argument,"[115] so do not get into one. The reality is that if you criticize people, shame them and make them feel wrong, they will resent you and dig into their position, not change it.

4 Carnegie does not tell people to shy away from disagreement—he just advises that we should not be argumentative. In one of the principles, "How to Criticize—and Not Be Hated for It,"[116] Carnegie says to be kind when you criticize. I worked with an HR director who used the "Oreo cookie method" of delivering criticism—praise, constructive feedback, then more praise. Frankly, that seemed more like a shit sandwich to me. All I heard was, "You generally are doing a good job, but you are doing these other things wrong, and we know you can improve, because you are such a valuable worker." None of the employees I tried it with felt good after an Oreo cookie session. Carnegie's way is more nuanced. He says to deliver the constructive feedback in a way that is positive. For example, "You are a good worker, who does a good job, and we have some ideas for how you can raise your performance even higher." In my experience, Carnegie's method is better. The worker tends to take the suggestion and improve his or her performance.

5 In the principle titled, "A Sure Way of Making Enemies—and How to Avoid It,"[117] Carnegie quotes Galileo, who said, "You cannot teach a man anything; you can only help him find it within himself."[118] Carnegie goes on to say that you should never tell someone else they are wrong. You can

disagree with them and explain why you see it differently, but do not tell them they are wrong.

If you view different opinions through a generational lens, it may help you see their perspective. For example, a Boomer, who has been in the workforce for a couple of decades, probably has fixed ideas about how people should dress in the office. A Millennial, who was brought up with different socially acceptable practices, will likely disagree and may feel constrained by the Boomer's ideas about dress code.

I am not saying all differences are about someone's generation; however, it is a lens through which we can view situations that helps us understand people better. Think of it like a Snapchat lens.[119] Listening to peoples' perspectives and thinking about it based on the era in which they were raised is like applying an augmented reality experience to a video. It shows us a different view.

6   One of my favorites is Carnegie's "A Formula that Will Work Wonders for You."[120] He says that we need to try to see the other person's point of view. He argues that we are more effective when we can see both sides of an argument.

7   In "What Everybody Wants,"[121] Carnegie talks again about understanding other people. He explains that being sympathetic goes a long way towards winning over people to our point of view.

8   "No One Likes to Take Orders"[122]—Carnegie was onto something with this one. Even if you are the boss, do not be bossy.

9   This is my favorite, because it speaks to exactly why America is so divided in the social media era: "Let the Other Person Save Face."[123] Carnegie says that if you must criticize someone, do it in private.

He says that nothing is more shameful than being criticized in front of a large group of people.

To Dale Carnegie, a tweet was the sound a bird makes, not a 280-character shame bomb lobbed across the internet for the world to read on a social media app called Twitter. But his prescription for how to treat others continues to hold up today.

The axioms listed above are not all of Dale Carnegie's 30 principles, but they give you the general idea. It is nearly 100 years later, and Dale Carnegie & Associates continues Carnegie's teachings today with a learning institute that features in-person and online courses. Why? Because the circumstances of our lives change and human beings can up level their understanding of life and the world around them, but our biology does not change. People react defensively to each other today, just as they did 100 years ago, and just as they will 100 years from now, which is why Carnegie's teachings withstand the test of time.

I will say this several times in this book, because if people take away anything, I want it to be this: Intolerance met with intolerance only leads to more intolerance.

CHAPTER 5 | OUR PARADOX: THE CHANGES ARE BOTH GOOD AND BAD

During a recent production shoot, my Gen X friend, an entertainment executive and entrepreneur, who has run her own successful business for more than 10 years now, instructed her Gen Z intern to ride in a van with an older white male director. Her thinking was that the 20-year-old intern, who is studying filmmaking in college, would benefit from a long drive in Los Angeles traffic with an experienced, award-winning director.

After a 15-hour day and a successful shoot, she was driving home when a realization hit her like a lightning bolt: She had just put her entire company—everything she has worked for—in jeopardy.

In her own words, "Hashtag 2019—you can't put a 20-year-old female intern in a van with a male executive alone. It jeopardizes both parties by implication."

Something that we would not have thought twice about in the 1980s or 1990s is now something powerful enough that it could take down a company.

The next day in the office, she was talking with her office manager about the production shoot and said, "I think I did something stupid yesterday when I let our intern ride with our director. I didn't even think about the implication of that on either side."

Without missing a beat, the office manager—a Millennial—

replied with her quick instinct, "Yeah, when you did it, I got a bad feeling in the pit of my stomach."

The good news here is that nothing happened. The reality check is that my friend's business instinct is from a bygone era. We have two generations in the workforce who are highly sensitized to issues of gender disparity, sexual misconduct and equality.

We taught certain values to the younger generations. We did a good thing when we did that. Corporate America was (and still is) riddled with all sorts of problematic behavior. But now it is incumbent on us to figure out how to incorporate these young adults and their values into a world that has not recognized those values and often does not understand them.

I have had conversations with Baby Boomer executives who think it is a problem that these younger generations are so sensitive, because senior level men, who can help these women in their careers, will no longer take a meeting alone with a woman. There are men who are refusing to travel on business with female colleagues. If these male managers do not mentor up-and-coming female workers, how will these women learn business and who will champion them to higher positions of power and authority within organizations?

Today, when men tell me that they do not feel comfortable with women in the workplace, I reply that being afraid of women and not supporting their advancement is not the answer. Truthfully, what I usually say is, "The answer is simple. Just don't be a creep."

Guys, you are saying that, if you cannot relax and be yourself at work, you would rather take all of your toys and play only with the other boys. If we think about it rationally, there should not be a problem here. A good rule of thumb in business is this: If you would not say it to your mother, sister or daughter, then do not say it to your female colleagues.

I realize that is all easier said than done. We get comfortable with the people with whom we work. Business colleagues become our work family. We are in the trenches together and go through business wars together. At times, we can feel closer to and better understood by our work colleagues than our own families. I get it. I have been there. AND times are changing, so we need to reassess how we show up in our work friendships.

Throughout our lives, we have different types of relationships. We have childhood friends, college friends, business friends, next-door-neighbor friends, friends we develop through our children, family and more. We show up differently in these relationships. Women being empowered to speak up at work and in life does not mean that men should abandon working with women. It means that it is time for Americans to reconsider how we behave in the workplace.

The reality is that this change—men being concerned about working with women—has created a paradox, because we ALL learn from people in business who have more experience than us. Are we really saying that the women have to stick with the women and the men have to stick with the men? In the simplest terms, that will not work. It does not benefit the employees, so it does not benefit corporate America.

Think about every male dominated institution, company and government that has allowed women to enter. Someone had to show them the ropes. If it was a male dominated organization, then obviously men were the ones to teach and mentor the women.

Using the example of my friend, who put a young female intern alone in a car with the male executive, it was a great opportunity for the intern to ask questions and have an uninterrupted conversation with an experienced director whom she most likely would not have had access to in an office or production setting; and that is exactly what happened. They had a great conversation and the director was impressed with the intern. Someday, he may hire her for a job thanks to that situation.

The Solution Is to Be More Human

In the Chinese Yin Yang symbol, you need both the black and the white halves contrasting each other in order to create the whole—this symbolizes the dual nature of life. If the women can only stick with the women and the men only with the men, we are not creating businesses and products that incorporate the whole of who we are as human beings. Right now, everyone—both young and old—seems to be having trouble allowing people to be human.

Some young women fly off the handle when they think an older male boss is "mansplaining" something to them, or they file a complaint with HR when a male colleague is friendly, and they deem it as being overly friendly. Some people are just overly friendly with no hidden agenda. But if a situation makes young adults uncomfortable at work or in school, they report it. The problem is that life is full of uncomfortable moments. Not all of them are an HR infraction.

For their part, older workers (both men and women) say demeaning things about these young adults just entering the workforce. They put them down, call them entitled, irrational, naive and hypersensitive. The older generations often dismiss the younger people's concerns and feelings.

The problem with that is we have spent hundreds of years disregarding how our words and actions affect other people. Yet the 2000s have been marked by enlightenment (currently known as being "woke"), as people wake up to the damage we have mindlessly done to the environment, to other animals and organisms, and especially to each other.

The difficult thing for many people to see is that both sides of the argument are right, because each generation sees it through their own lens of experience. The current paradox of right and right means that neither opinion is wrong. If you can follow that, you are a genius, because heads are spinning in HR departments throughout the country as they react to this intergenerational conflict and the dramatic shift in what is acceptable behavior and what is not.

The solution to the paradox is not for us to be less human, or point fault, but to be more human. We need to better understand each other so we can move forward. We live in a world where social media acts as a megaphone for people to express their opinions on what they see. Technology and changing societal attitudes have propelled us into a necessary correction in how we relate in business (and in life). However, some of what is happening is an overcorrection.

Let me give you an example of what I mean. I teach a graduate level class at Columbia University in corporate communications. Recently, during a class session about giving speeches, a student delivered a short speech he had written, in which he told a personal and revealing story. When we went around the room giving feedback on the speech, many of the students commented that the story made them uncomfortable and they thought he should not use it in the speech. I remarked that the purpose of a speech is to make people think, not to make them comfortable. Some of the most famous speeches throughout history are memorable precisely because they made people uncomfortable—they compelled us to take action.

When I said that, several of the students' eyes grew wide in disbelief. How could I possibly say that it is acceptable, in fact advisable, to make people feel uncomfortable? It was as if I had introduced a completely foreign concept to them.

There are innumerable examples on college and high school campuses of students requiring more sensitivity from professors and administrators. Students are demanding that schools be more aware of issues around race, gender, sexuality and mental health. The students are right. For too long, people have been insensitive to the needs and feelings of marginalized groups.

While this started as a necessary improvement, it quickly leapfrogged into overcorrection territory. As schools scramble to adjust to the needs of their students, many professors and administrators are critical of the current hypersensitivity. They rightfully argue that free-speech discourse, debate and critical thinking are vital skills taught in academia, and students need to be more tolerant of their own discomfort.

In one such example, a fiery issue at Yale became a national story in 2015 after the administration sent an email asking students to be mindful of cultural misappropriation during Halloween. A subsequent email from a professor of early childhood education pointed out the paradox and questioned if the Yale community had become overly sensitive and was squelching free speech.[124] In her email, Professor Erika Christakis said, "Free speech and the ability to tolerate offence are the hallmarks of a free and open society."[125] The professor's email and a subsequent op-ed in the *Yale Herald* written by a student kicked off a national shitstorm with critics on both sides of the issue.

This is another case where both sides of the argument are right, which is the modern-day paradox where change is both good and bad. If both sides are right and nobody is wrong, how do we come to an understanding?

I do not pretend to have the answer to that question, but I certainly have a few ideas about how we can fix it. Let's start with mitigating the public blame-and-shame game that happens daily, which I will explore in the next chapter.

CHAPTER 6 | THE TOXIC SHAME-BLAME GAME

As Millennials entered their twenties and thirties, they showed up as a powerful force advocating for equality and fairness for all genders and races. Millennials are not the first generation to fight for these ideals; however, at 71 million, they are one of the largest generations to do it.[126] They can also express themselves on social media, which makes it possible for everyone to have a voice and to reach a broad public audience.

Throughout history, there have been societal practices that were not acceptable, but they were accepted. In the United States, two of those practices were slavery and a patriarchal society that denied women the right to vote. Additionally, throughout history, young people have spoken out when they deemed a societal practice to be unfair and unjust. In the 1800s, Susan B. Anthony was in her twenties when she started working as an abolitionist and a daring advocate of women's rights.[127] Martin Luther King, Jr. was just 34 years old when he delivered his famous "I Have a Dream" speech in 1963.[128]

With that in mind, let's look at the workplace and some examples of things that were not acceptable but were accepted. My mother started working on Wall Street in the 1960s. Women in the offices of the big banks used to let each other know which guys were "handsy" and which were safe. As my mom says, "You made sure to stay on your side of his desk and not to be left alone with him." She went on to have a 50-year career on Wall Street and retired at the age of 77 from JP Morgan.

My mom was one of the first women to pave a way for others, and yet, you still do not see a lot of older women on Wall Street. Why? Because old-school attitudes in banking and finance make it difficult for women to have children and a career in that field. My mom made sacrifices to have the career she had. In the office, she chose to dress conservatively, and she made sure to work for safe men—she had the luxury of being able to do that. As a parent, she was not one of the moms who attended every play, music recital or sporting event, because she could not leave the office if the stock market was open.

I entered the business world in the 1980s and 1990s. As a result of the women's movement, women had more sexual freedom and entitlement, albeit not much authority in business. Some women exercised their sexual freedom in ways that would be completely unacceptable today. It was a different era and we had a different understanding of the world. For example, when I was in my twenties and thirties, I did not dress conservatively, like my mother did. In fact, if I was wearing something low cut as I left the house, my then-husband Brian would supportively wish me good luck on getting approval for whatever I needed from my male boss that day. He was right to make that joke-not-a-joke. I stopped wearing low-cut clothing when I was in my mid-thirties, because it was not who I wanted to be as I got older. But in my twenties, using my femininity felt empowering.

Similarly, when I was a junior executive, it used to be a thing for people to bring a boyfriend, girlfriend—or a co-worker—back to the office after a night of cocktails at a nearby bar and have sex on a desk. After all, this was the era of *Moonlighting*—and other TV shows like it—where working together and having sexual tension, or flat-out sexual relationships, were in vogue. Maybe it still happens today, and I do not hear about it. But, 30 years ago, single friends would gossip with each other about their sexcapades at work.

Some women felt emboldened by their sexuality and acted on it. Other women had the opposite experience. They were harassed and abused simply for being female.

Different era = Different understanding of sex and women's empowerment = Different morals = Different socially accepted behaviors.

I am grateful that the #MeToo movement has arrived. For decades, women only told close friends about the sexual improprieties of powerful men in their industries. If these women dared to speak up and tell someone in authority, they were often not believed unless they had proof of the impropriety. Even then—with proof or without it—the woman's role at the company was marginalized, and she was eventually fired.

However, I think we are in a moment when women have gotten into the habit of crying, "Off with their heads!" at every minor male indiscretion. This is why it can be helpful to look at these situations through a generational lens. Our attitudes, opinions and lifestyle are shaped by the era in which we were raised. As a result, sexual behaviors that were not acceptable, but used to be accepted, are not accepted in today's more woke environment.

I realize that last line is a bit of a brain twister. Bottom line, what was accepted in the 1900s is not accepted in the 2000s. Let's look at two well-known cases of men who resigned after #MeToo controversies: Al Franken (born 1951), who is a comedian, author, producer and former Democratic Senator from Minnesota; and former CBS CEO Leslie Moonves (born 1949), whom I worked for at CBS and CBS-owned companies for over 10 years.

What happened? In 2017, Franken voluntarily resigned from the Senate after a female reporter accused him of inappropriate groping and kissing during a USO Tour that took place in 2006. Moonves stepped down from CBS in 2018 after multiple women accused him of sexual misconduct in the 1980s and 1990s. Ronan Farrow wrote two stories for *The New Yorker* that led to an investigation by the CBS Board of Directors and Moonves' resignation.

Now, let us consider their conditioning as Baby Boomers and men working in Hollywood. Franken started as a writer and performer on *Saturday Night Live* in the 1970s and 80s, where they pushed the boundaries around sex and language on late-night television. Moonves started his career as an actor and worked as an assistant to a casting agent in the early 1970s. Both of these men came of age in the pre-feminist, "Mad Men" era, which was later popularized by the AMC drama of the same name. Behaving chauvinistically was a sign of power in business and was part of the male conditioning at that time. I would argue that it was an unacceptable behavior that was nonetheless an accepted practice for decades. (In some businesses, it is still an accepted practice.)

As a result of that conditioning, men—and women—in the 1960s grew up with different rules about sexuality, gender roles and power than people are taught today. This is a good example of why using the generational lens is helpful when considering another person's perspective.

In 2019, Kim Masters of *The Hollywood Reporter* filed an editorial about whether or not the "Time's Up movement" had gone too far or not far enough.[129] [The Time's Up movement is presumably named after the eponymous organization that was formed in the wake of the #MeToo movement to serve as a watchdog protecting women and calling out abusive men and the companies that enable them.]

Masters has written several investigative pieces exposing sexual harassment and abuse in Hollywood, so she has had a frontline seat to female allegations of abuse and the corporate antics that happen just before the abuses are about to be made public in a media story. Masters concluded that the Time's Up movement had not gone far enough, because women continue to be silenced with payouts and the media companies continue to protect these men.

My hypothesis is that Time's Up and the #MeToo movement have gone as far as they can, because the current environment of toxic blaming and shaming is not working. Abusers dig into their positions, feeling resentful for being misunderstood and judged. Victims do not feel vindicated, because the abusers are not remorseful. Meanwhile, society is missing critical opportunities to inform and reform.

In the *Hollywood Reporter* editorial, Masters says that she had hope for how Louis C.K. (who is a member of Gen X) would handle his #MeToo problem. "I thought he might vanish for a year, look inward (as he promised) and come back with insight."[130]

Louis C.K. (in)famously went back to the comedy circuit less than a year after being accused of masturbating in front of unwilling women. He performed in smaller clubs with a set that attacked political correctness, along with various ethnic and cultural groups. Detractors have said he showed an incredible lack of self-awareness in his first routines post his #MeToo downfall.

Some people have done bad things and deserve to lose their jobs and, in some cases, go to jail. Others have done misguided things and need to be better informed about why their behavior was problematic. Not everything is a fireable offense. As human beings, we all do the best we can with the information we have and the experiences we have.

Can a white male, who has been in a position of power, truly understand what it is like to be a woman and be powerless? I do not think so. I have advanced degrees in psychology and have studied this. I think men can logically understand the concept of a female—the "fairer sex"—being powerless. However, many of them do not truly comprehend it because, as adult males in the workforce, very few of them have ever physically experienced that sense of powerlessness.

Do you know the expression, "Walk a mile in my shoes"? Well, this is the epitome of it.

Can a man know what it is like to be a female? Can a white male know what it is like to be an African American, Latino or Asian man? Can anyone who has grown up with privilege know what it is like to be poor? No, they cannot. They can feel empathy, because they can imagine what it is like to be in that experience. But until they actually experience it, they do not really know what it is like.

Academy Award®-winning filmmaker and co-founder of Miramax, Harvey Weinstein, is arguably the most well-known and notorious case of sexual abuse in the #MeToo era. At least 87 women have accused Weinstein of sexual abuse and harassment.[131] He was convicted in February 2020 of committing a criminal sex

act and third-degree rape.[132] Aside from the conviction, Weinstein's actions have been publicly derided and the publicity
around him is helping corporate America to change for the better.

But there are all types of transgressions that do not rise to
that level and we are at risk of overcorrecting if we treat them
all the same way. We cannot lead a movement where all men are
bad—some incidents are simple misunderstandings, some are misguided mistakes, and some are gross transgressions. It is a huge
challenge to navigate since these situations often come down to
he-said-she-said. However, it can be done when the intentions for
truth and fairness are in place.

Intolerance Met with Intolerance Only Leads to More Intolerance

Real change does not come from people on opposite sides
of an issue hurling nasty grams over a virtual fence, a.k.a., Twitter.
Real change does not come from pundits talking over each other
on the 24-hour news channels. What we are experiencing right
now is an up leveling of our society. We are in a massive teaching moment. Whether it is gun violence, sexual harassment and
assault, equal pay for women, discrimination against non-whites,
LGBTQ rights and more, we have an opportunity to educate and
inform. That does not happen when we blame and shame. Being
bullied makes people defensive and they then become more en-
trenched in their beliefs, not less so.

There are some people who do not feel remorse for their actions. There are people who conduct themselves in a way in which
they feel justified and they defend themselves vehemently. They
do not see where their words and actions are damaging to others.
As human beings, we often judge other people by how we would
behave in a similar situation. But we are all different.

For example, U.S. President Donald Trump (a Baby Boomer) and aforementioned movie mogul Harvey Weinstein (also a
Boomer) have both been accused by multiple women of sexual
harassment and assault. Both of them have strongly defended

their behaviors and claimed that the interactions with their female accusers were consensual. Meanwhile, other men accused of sexual harassment or lesser indisgressions have apologized, gone to therapy, or otherwise tried to learn from their hurtful attitudes and actions. Academy Award®-winning actor Casey Affleck[133] (from Generation X) and former New York Attorney General Eric Schneiderman[134] (a Boomer) are two examples of this.

The psychological reality of being a human being is that we see life differently, because we all have different experiences. To that point, some people have a capacity for empathy, while others have a level of narcissism that makes it impossible for them to understand or accept someone else's perspective. In some cases, people can have a clinical level of narcissism.

If you look up Narcissistic "Personality Disorders" in the *Diagnostic and Statistical Manual of Mental Disorders, 5th ed.*, which is the diagnostic guide used by licensed therapists and psychologists to classify different mental health issues, you will find that its criteria include oppressive behavior, entitlement, conceit and a lack of empathy, among others.[135] Only a licensed professional with an advanced degree in psychology can accurately diagnose a client to determine if the level of narcissism is clinical. The rest of it is just speculation on social media, opinion news shows, and late night television.

Twitter, in particular, is a polarizing platform where the Twitterati hurl accusations and engage in name calling during vitriolic attacks on people who are not definitively on their side of an issue. It is very easy to attack people when we are not face-to-face with them. Many times, the tone and nature of the conversation is completely different when we are physically in a room with the other person. Human beings are more complex than the Twitter bully pulpit allows. Empathy, compassion and understanding are what distinguish human beings from other animals—and from artificial intelligence.

As a human being—with all of our complexity of emotions—both of the sentiments I have expressed can co-exist: It is possible for me to support women and be grateful to them for

speaking up, while still having empathy for friends and colleagues—like Leslie Moonves—who have learned lessons about
respecting women and behaving reasonably.

The haters on Twitter may have a field day with that statement, but I believe that if we are going to co-exist peacefully, we
need to get back to allowing each other to be human. These are important events that can be teaching moments, not a tennis match
of toxic blaming and shaming. I guarantee you that no one has
all of the information—not the best reporter or the best investigative journalist, and certainly not the armchair quarterback with a
Twitter account.

CHAPTER 7 | HOW TO EMBRACE CHANGE AND WHY WE RESIST IT

The discussion in the previous chapter tees up perfectly a fundamental fact about human psychology: People see the world through their own lens. A lot of research has been done on this. When the police interview people immediately following an accident, multiple witnesses will describe the same incident differently. Details can differ dramatically ranging from the cause of the crash to the make and model of the cars and color of the clothing worn by the people involved.

Is this because the witnesses were not paying attention? No! The witnesses were fully present. In a trauma, such as watching a car crash unfold, the fight, flight or freeze portion of our brains kick in, our bodies are flooded with stress hormones, and our brains light up with activity as we process what we are experiencing.

The reason for the differences in witness recollection is because, as human beings, we have a filter that is so pervasive that we do not even know it is there. In life, everything that happens to us is filtered through every experience and emotion we have ever had prior to that moment.

The ancient Toltec wisdom teachings say that human beings go through life in a dream state. We all see life through our own filter of emotions and past experiences, so it is the same as a living dream. (If you want to know more about the Toltec teachings, it is explained thoroughly by Don Miguel Ruiz in his two *New York Times* Best-Selling books, *The Four Agreements* and *The Fifth Agreement*.)

There is also a modern, scientific explanation of the same idea, thanks to neuroscience. The amygdala is an almond-shaped mass of cells that lives in a deep part of our brain. It is responsible for our automatic responses known as fight, flight or freeze during periods of stress. It drives many of our primary emotions, such as fear, anger, and pleasure. In its very important role, the amygdala dictates our motivations—automatically and unconsciously.

When an event happens, the amygdala dictates how big our emotional response is going to be. Imagine that you have a thermometer inside your head. When something happens to you that causes your stress or fear to rise from a level one to a level 10, the imaginary thermometer turns red and bursts. Hitting a 10 on the imaginary stress thermometer kicks off a series of events in the brain—the amygdala is now in charge; the limbic system takes over the brain and the prefrontal cortex shuts down.

Here is the problem with that situation. First, it happens to all of us without us knowing it. No one escapes this brain phenomena. Second, the prefrontal cortex is responsible for executive functioning. Executive functioning is exactly as it sounds. It is the part of the brain that makes rational decisions, problem solves and exerts self-control.

Let me say that again—at certain levels of stress or distress, the amygdala shuts down self-control and the part of the brain responsible for our subconscious programming takes over. No one can escape this biological reality.

Unconscious Bias

That was a very simplified version of a complex process that has many more moving parts than what I described. The key point is that both Toltec wisdom and neuroscience are saying the same thing, which is that human beings see life through a filter. We make snap decisions about what we like and do not like without being conscious of it. We then act on those decisions quickly and decisively without questioning their origins. We are certain in our convictions. But those convictions are based on a story that has built up in our brains over decades of life experiences.

Bottom line: The only reality that exists is our own reality. The one created by our mind's experiences.

Because of this, we believe what we believe. Further to that, in the U.S. we have a constitution that says we have the unalienable right to life, liberty and the pursuit of happiness. We also have freedom of speech, freedom of the press, freedom of religion, freedom of petition and freedom of peaceful assembly, according to the First Amendment.

As Americans, we are allowed to believe what we believe and be who we are, whether we are the victim, the accused or the angry pundit shouting our opinion on Twitter, Fox News Channel, or CNN.

Going back to sexual harassment as an example of the changes happening thanks to these younger generations, I have spoken to many female friends about the #MeToo movement. We all agree that it is about time. But we do not all agree that it is being handled fairly. Some of my female friends say, "An eye for an eye." Women were harassed, subjugated and held back for centuries. It is our turn! Still other female friends say things have gone too far. Like any correction, they believe the #MeToo movement has become an overcorrection.

Both of these opinions are allowed in our society and are ratified by our constitution. It is time to get back to allowing the individual to be an individual.

Obviously, if someone breaks the law, they should have a fair trial and go to jail if found guilty. That is Amendment VI of the Bill of Rights. Defendants have the right to a public trial with an impartial jury. That is a beautiful part of being American. However, what happens when the person's actions are immoral and unethical, but not illegal?

Since 2017, some very public and powerful men in Hollywood—actors, filmmakers, and executives—have lost their jobs because women are emboldened to speak. But the Entertainment Industry is not the only business sector that allowed men to subjugate women—I am looking at you, Finance, Medicine, Manufacturing, Academia, and many others.

In a patriarchal society, like the United States, men used to have all the power and women were not heard. Thanks to social media and the values parents have instilled in their Millennial and Gen Z children, the rules have changed. Equality, fairness and transparency are core values to these two generations. But fairness goes both ways.

We have become a society driven by toxic shame. We jump to quick conclusions, publicly shame people, and serve as judge and jury in the court of public opinion, all within minutes on social media. There is no room for making mistakes. There is no opportunity for teaching moments. There is no time for learning what we did wrong, apologizing and being forgiven.

No matter what side of the moral argument we are on—conservative or liberal, Democrat or Republican—when we are intolerant, we are no better than the people we are fighting against.

This blaming and shaming thing we are doing is not working. Political polls in the past few years suggest that Americans do not agree on much, except that we do not like how polarized our country is at this moment.

Our forefathers disagreed vehemently about the best way to structure our government and the language in the constitution. So how is it that they were able to arrive at a compromise to create, what we now know as, the United States Constitution? They listened to each other. They took the time to understand the other side's perspective. And they compromised in the name of the greatest good for all.

They also challenged each other to duels and shot each other at dawn. Thankfully, we do not do that anymore. But we have developed the modern-day equivalent by vilifying people in the court of public opinion on social media and online forums.

Listening and understanding are what has helped our

country become a superpower. Intolerance and toxic shaming are tearing it down.

Where Do We Go from Here?

Like the financial markets during a bubble, there is always an overcorrection that brings stock prices, corporate earnings and consumer spending down to earth. In business right now, people are having trouble relating to each other in a way that we have not seen since the Hippie counterculture movement of the 1960s. While older generations do not see the problem, younger generations only see the problem. The changes that are permeating our society and businesses are like a cancer that older workers do not realize is eating companies from the inside out.

We currently have five generations in the workforce—Silent Generation, Baby Boomers, Gen X, Millennials and Gen Z. Think about those differences for a minute. The way an 18-year-old views the world is very different from the way an 80-year-old views the world.

The reason I focus so much on the #MeToo movement in this book is because a lot of people say it is responsible for dividing us by gender. In my view, the differences in opinion are also a generational issue. When many younger Millennials (ages 24 to early 30s) and Gen Zers (ages 10 to 23) watch old TV series, such as "Seinfeld," they find them offensive. They cannot believe that there was a period when we thought it was entertaining to make fun of people's handicaps, shortcomings and differences.

These younger generations are more attuned to letting individuals be individuals. They do not just value diversity, they expect it, because their lives are full of diversity. Whether it is ethnic, racial, spiritual or gender differences, Millennials and Gen Z are the most diverse population the U.S. has ever had—Millennials are 56 percent white and 44 percent other ethnicities, while Gen Z is 50 percent white and 50 percent other ethnicities.[136]

How Companies Change

There are certain fundamental truths about human beings and how they deal with change. If you attended business school, you likely learned about the J Curve.[137] It is an observed academic theory that has been applied to economics, business operations, politics and even medicine. There are many ways to apply the J-Curve theory, so let's look at an example that involves corporate finance. (This will not be as painful as that made it sound.)

The J Curve posits that a business, economy or government in transition will go through a period of losses—a downturn—before it then returns to a period of growth. On a chart with an x- and y-axis, this phenomenon plots out like the letter "J." Ergo, the name of the theory: The J Curve.

For example, in private equity, when a company receives an infusion of cash from venture capital, the company then experiences a period of financial losses as it deploys the new capital. After that period of loss, also known as "spending money in order to make money," the company eventually returns to a period of growth. Or so the theory says.

The J Curve can also be applied to businesses in transition. A good example is print media. As I mentioned in an earlier chapter, readership of printed newspapers and glossy magazines is declining as more people are getting their news and magazine content online and on social media. This is a major disruption to newspaper and magazine publishers, who have had to completely rethink their business models and ways of making money.

As the publishing business restructures, revenues go down as these companies rebuild their businesses. Once the restructurings are done, the new business lines grow (hopefully), operations start to bring in more revenue, and economies of scale kick in to drive profit.

While the J Curve is about financial loss and gain, it is a period in a company's lifespan that causes a lot of uncertainty and stress for employees! It is vital at these points for the C-suite executives, especially the CEO, Chief Human Resources Officer and

Chief Communications Officer, to pay more attention than ever to corporate culture.

When a company is experiencing a J Curve, it is a key time to regularly measure employee sentiment—I call it "taking the temperature of the company." A quick quarterly assessment of how employees view the company and their jobs enables leaders to institute changes that will help attract and retain good talent. Everyone thinks that a company's primary business is its product or service. I argue that the company's primary business is its human capital. Companies employ people, but it is the people who run the company. Therefore, employees are a company's most important asset!

The reason a J-Curve period will cause problems for employees is the same reason that any change causes problems in the life of an organization—people resist change!

Why is that? The quick answer is that we are wired that way.

Grab the Caffeine, Because We're Going to Talk about Neuroscience Again

There is a lot written about how human beings are wired and a lot of it is verbose academic theory and medical jargon. But if you go to *Psychology Today*, which writes accessible articles and blog posts for non-scientists, you will find over 4,000 articles on "resistance to change."

There are many reasons why human beings resist change and the degree to which we avoid change varies from person to person. Your individual upbringing makes you who you are, and it is why we are all different.

Everything you experience goes into the vegetable soup that defines who you are. These factors include:

- Your parents' beliefs, which you either accept or reject.

- Your parents' relationship—was there violence in the home or was it a Brady Bunch-like household?

- Where you went to school—was it public or private; religious; diverse or homogenous?

- The town you grew up in—was it conservative, liberal, small, large, urban or suburban?

- The language you speak—the word "love" in English means strong affection for. In Japanese, love has many different meanings and there are different words to account for all of the nuances, so you better use the right one when you are first getting to know someone!

- The religion you were given (or not given) by your families.

- The life philosophies you learned (positive or negative) by friends, family and teachers.

- The events in your neighborhood and country while you were growing up—in the U.S. in the 1950s, children were taught in school how to duck and cover in case of a nuclear attack. In the 1980s, these practices were stopped, since they were deemed to be futile and believed to make people complacent about the nuclear threat. Those are two different worldviews about nuclear war that shaped two different generations.

This is not an exhaustive list. It is only a few examples of the things that make us who we are.

Experience informs every decision that human beings make in life. Our brains and central nervous systems operate on cause-and-effect learning. So, the conscious reasons for why we resist change are related to the experiences we had as children, which guide us as adults.

However, in general, it is almost universal that human beings like things that make us feel secure and comfortable, and resist things that make us uncomfortable. This biological truth makes us prone to habitual behavior and it comes from neuroscience.

As mentioned earlier, the reptilian brain (its medical name is basal ganglia) controls many functions, but it is most notably responsible for our body's primitive drives, like the need for safety, food and sex. It also controls repetitive activities and habits—think: driving, brushing our teeth, biting our nails, and a host of other things we "do without thinking."[138]

While the J-Curve discussion may have seemed like a bit of a tangent, it is important to the point of this chapter, which is that change is inevitable, and yet we are wired to resist it.[139] Our reptilian brain makes snap decisions without us even knowing it and it is why human beings have an unconscious, negative response to change.

Obviously, if our brains are trained toward habit and act defensively to change, that makes transformations in business a big problem. Moreover, I would argue that the shift that is happening in corporate America, as a result of Millennials and Gen Z joining the workforce, is not a transformation, it is a revolution.

Now, you may say that you miss the good old days when life seemed more leisurely and the pace of change was slower. I get that. Business and life today seem to move at an unrelenting speed thanks to advances in technology. But the problem with today's advances are not the shifts they create, but our ability to adjust to them. It is the discomfort of the adjustment that leads us to resist it.

The Dalai Lama wrote in his book, *The Art of Happiness*, that human beings are pleasure seeking beings and we all want the same thing, which is happiness and freedom from suffering.[140] Some people find it really difficult to embrace change. That does not mean it is impossible, it just means it is difficult.

Some people are better at accepting change than others. I learned from a master to grab onto change and ride it to success. I mentioned earlier that Dawn Ostroff has been my boss at three different companies. She is a media executive with a keen eye for trends and an ability to embrace and lead change in a disruptive environment.

Dawn also told me that I should always ask for what I want, because the worst thing someone can say to me is, "No." That question can be personal, such as, "Can I take the week off?" It can be professional, such as, "I have worked hard and proven myself. Can I have a raise and promotion?" Or it can be about business, such as, "I have an idea for how we can change this process. Can we try it?" No matter what the question is, I always ask it, and

Dawn was right, the answer is always some form of yes or no.

Knowing that we are resistant to change biologically goes a long way to helping us accept change, which is inevitable. In fact, it is something that we want and need. Without change, life becomes stagnant. There are countless business books and self-help/life hack books to help people change. What is important to know here is that change can be good. At the very least, change is inevitable.

Self-knowledge is important for understanding our reactions to life. When you know that you think and act a certain way, and you want to change your beliefs or actions, you can then take proactive measures to retrain your brain through repetitive steps that are different from what you usually do. So, if you become defensive and dig into your position when someone suggests that you do something differently at work, try taking a deep breath and repeating a mantra, such as, "Change is good. I am excited to see what it brings."

If that sounds hokey, then pick your own mantra. And, if you have trouble remembering it, put the mantra in a reminder on your phone and set it to go off once every few hours. I live by my iPhone's Reminders app. I have used it for years to help retrain my brain to think in different ways.

CHAPTER 8 | RIDING THE WAVE OF THE CULTURAL REVOLUTION

Now that we have looked at why it is hard for people—and therefore companies—to change, we can examine what needs to be done to ride the wave of the cultural revolution that Millennials and Gen Z are leading. As discussed in an earlier chapter, the Great Recession in 2008 affected all of us, but if you want to understand why young adults have little interest in jobs in corporate America, you need look no further than how old they were when that recession hit.

Older Millennials had just entered the workforce or were in college looking for full-time work in 2008. Meanwhile, the oldest Gen Zers were in junior high school and watched their parents and other family members struggle through the Great Recession. In both cases, these younger cohorts learned two key lessons. First, corporate America cannot be depended upon for job security. Second, the stock market is the real-life version of Mr. Toad's Wild Ride at Disney World.

The results are predictable now that we are all living them. Here's a recap:

1   At this stage of their lifecycle, many Millennials are financially behind previous generations. Many still depend on their parents or grandparents for help.[141] It is too early to tell if Gen Z will be financially impacted by midlife.

2   Many Millennials and Gen Zers prefer the gig
economy to office jobs. They want more freedom
than a traditional 9-to-5 job allows for, and freelance work enables them to also take care of their
personal interests.

3   As discussed, their prevailing attitude around
working full time is that if they stay at a job for
longer than 18 to 24 months, there is something
wrong with them—as in, they are not good
enough to find another job. For Gen X and Boomers, if we moved around too much there was
something wrong with us. This new way of thinking is a major change. It also means these young
adults walk out the door after companies have
taken the time and resources to train them, but
before they have realized a return on that investment.

4   Neither generation trusts the stock market. They
would sooner invest in a friend's startup or put
their money under a mattress.[142]

To put their situation into perspective, we are talking about
two generations that experienced a global economic crisis just as
they were seriously considering what they wanted to be when
they grew up. At the same time, the federal government lowered
interest rates to historic lows in order to juice the economy, which
made their mattress or the piggy bank as good an investment as a
savings account.

And who can blame them? This is a perfectly rational
response to a long and painful recession, which happened when
they were at very impressionable stages as kids and young people
just entering the workforce.

Another problem for corporate America is that more people today are getting college and advanced degrees.[143] In theory
that should be a positive, but there are repercussions. We have a
more educated workforce that needs higher-income jobs to pay

off student loans. Also, their training and expectations are to work in professional settings, as opposed to earning hourly wages as unskilled laborers. Furthermore, they do not need corporate America to earn money. As previously stated, both generations, but especially Gen Z, have embraced the gig economy, freelancing and entrepreneurship.

Young Talent Is Hard to Recruit and Even Harder to Keep

Almost any employer will tell you right now that it is very difficult to recruit and retain good talent, while joining the cultural revolution and adapting to young adults is not that difficult. Let us look back at some of the workplace characteristics of Millennials and Gen Z and discuss how companies can adjust for them.

As stated, Millennials are motivated by fun, freedom and the opportunity to be involved. They want to work with a team, and they want to be part of the action. Recognition is important to them and it is not just about the "everybody gets a trophy" thing. They have a right to push for more responsibility, bigger titles and more money, because they are better trained and more educated than any generation before them. In addition, older workers are delaying retirement and are not letting go of their positions of power to make room for these younger generations.

As mentioned earlier, my mother worked on Wall Street for over 50 years. Given my role model, I have told my financial planner that I do not intend to retire. I plan to work for as long as my body and mind will allow. With older generations staying in the workforce longer, Millennials (and eventually Gen Z) are getting squeezed in the middle and it will take them longer to get to the top of the corporate food chain than it took the Baby Boomers.[144] This problem is also affecting Gen X's ability to advance in their careers.

Gen Z is success oriented.[145] This could make it seem like they are more driven than their Millennial cohort. First, Gen Z watched their parents suffer through the Great Recession, so they know that moving up the ladder is not as simple as climbing it one step at a time. Not surprisingly, they are attracted to careers that will weather a recession.[146] Also, they are being raised by Gen X, which values independence and resourcefulness, since they are a generation that was primarily left home alone. Finally, Gen Z has grown up in the best economy most Americans have ever seen and success is as easy as coming up with a good idea, using your smartphone to create it and deploying your social media channels to market it. Success is not easy, but it is prevalent when you are living in a boom economy.

Both generations want to find meaning in their work. This should not be misinterpreted as they only want to do jobs that save the world. Finding meaning in your work can come from doing something that you are good at and enjoy, like being a financial advisor specializing in teaching women to take control of their investing; crunching numbers to come up with the ideal price for a merger between two smaller healthcare companies that will result in a major power shift in that industry; or selling makeup that is not tested on animals.

Companies that do well recruiting and retaining young adult talent have a few things in common:

1   Management understands and respects the needs of their young adult workforce.

2   Management is transparent and communicates with employees.

3   Management listens to employees.

4   The organization's processes for raises, promotions and opportunities for professional growth are equitable and clear.

Is It Really That Simple?

Simple, yes. Easy, no. We are undergoing a cultural revolution and we are talking about changing the way most businesses in America function.

The first item on the list above—understanding and respecting the needs of your Millennial and Gen Z workers—means educating your older workers about the differences discussed in this book. To do that, you can bring in experts to help your company navigate the cultural revolution. Some companies hire corporate speakers to talk with their employees. Others engage corporate communications agencies and management consultants to guide them on how to establish corporate culture and better communicate with employees.

Next on the list is being transparent and using constant, clear communications. This is counter to the way most older managers have functioned in business for decades. In real estate, the mantra for success is "Location, location, location." In corporate America today, the mantra needs to be "Communicate, communicate, communicate."

For example, if there are rumors that your company is going to be bought by a competitor, you can call a company town hall and address the rumors. I am not saying that you should announce to your employees that a deal is inevitable. A lot of times, there are legal reasons why management cannot be forthcoming. But leaders can still tell the employees that they know the rumors are happening and that they will communicate with the staff as soon as they are able to do so. You can use the opportunity to talk about what a great year the company is having, or why its performance—and their hard work—has put the company in a place where its business is an attractive takeover target.

The third point just stated—listening to your young adult employees—is good for business and yet something that not a lot of organizations do, especially when older managers feel threatened by the changes that are happening. Listening to your younger workers has several benefits. It helps you identify opportunities to improve your business and alleviate issues that are keeping your staff from being fully productive. It also makes your employees feel valued and heard.

Finally, a lot of managers do not like to take risks and let go of control, so putting faith in young workers and giving them higher-level assignments is tough for micromanagers. But many Millennial and Gen Z workers thrive when consistently given the chance to take on more responsibility. At the very least, companies that offer a lot of opportunities for advancement with stated processes for raises and promotions that are clear and equitable have a better time retaining young workers.

As I said, the solution is simple, but it is not easy. We are talking about changing the way companies have operated for decades. It is the need to retrain your brain, but in this case, it is retraining the brain trust of the organization.

The four steps outlined above create a dynamic shift in how organizations operate. Businesses that do not take these steps risk becoming irrelevant and stagnant, because they will not be able to attract new talent to work for them. As I pointed out at the start of the book, Millennials are the largest generation in the workforce today[147] and Gen Z is the largest generation in the United States.[148] They are not going to adjust to us; we need to adjust to them.

CHAPTER 9 | COMING SOON: GENERATION ALPHA

While you may still think of Millennials as kids, the reality of it is that they are young adults heading into middle age, who are birthing our next generation, tentatively named Generation Alpha.

It is important to know that there is no consensus on this right now. As stated in an earlier chapter, I use Pew Research for my generational names and dates, and Pew has not yet determined the end of Generation Z. The primary expert talking about Generation Alpha is the well-known social researcher and author Mark McCrindle from Australia, whom I referenced in an earlier chapter.

McCrindle states that Generation Alpha was born starting in 2010 and they are the first generation to be wholly born and raised in the 21st century. He predicts that there are 9,000 Gen Alpha babies born to Millennial parents every day—that is 2.5 million a week. When all is said and done, in 2025, this generation will span nearly 2 billion worldwide.[149]

While it is hard for researchers to know a lot about a generation that is still figuring it out themselves, some assumptions can be made by looking at their parents. A few interesting facts about Millennials as parents—they often come from divorced homes and they are delaying marriage either to find the right partner or for financial reasons. The result is that the divorce rate in the U.S. is declining.[150] Additionally, Millennials are having fewer children, probably as a result of getting married later in life. *Psychology*

Today cites various studies, which show that birth rates among women in their twenties are declining, and, conversely, women in their early thirties are having children at higher rates than young women in their teens and twenties.[151]

Gen Alpha is growing up with older parents, who are more mature and better established financially. Gen Alpha also has fewer siblings, and many of them are only children. This generation will also be more ethnically diverse than their Millennial parents and Gen Z cohort. According to the U.S. Census Bureau, in 2011, more than 50 percent of babies were born to ethnically diverse families.[152]

Let us look at the world in which they are growing up. Gen Alpha is growing up with technology that is so pervasive it is not considered to be a tool, but "deeply integrated parts of everyday life."[153] It makes sense. The iPad was introduced in 2010, just as Gen Alpha was being born. Many of them intuitively figured out how to swipe left on a screen before they could walk. As a result, they heavily influence technology purchases by their parents and marketers are seizing on that, according to *AdAge*.[154] After all, companies know that the key to longevity is attracting consumers when we are young, because the brands we have an affinity for as adults are the brands that we used while growing up.

Who Gen Alpha Is in Their Own (Really Cute) Words

At this stage, it is obviously challenging to know what young kids will be like when they grow up, but that did not stop me from asking a group of 6-to-8-year-olds during a study I conducted with a third-party market research firm. The research company recruited a total of 11 boys and girls between the ages of six and eight years old, all of whom lived within driving distance of Woodbridge, New Jersey, where the focus group was held.

None of the children knew each other and they were recruited from a variety of schools with no more than two children attending the same school. The children came from diverse ethnic backgrounds as voluntarily identified by their parents, which included Hispanic, African American, Asian and Caucasian. They also had a variety of interests, which included watching TV (whether it be on a phone, tablet or television set), playing video games, competing in sports, attending school club activities and volunteering.

The focus group lasted for one hour and their parents were in the room with us. An assistant and I asked the children a variety of questions, which involved them answering individually, drawing pictures and circling answers on a sheet.

The entertainment industry will be pleased to know that all 11 of the children watch television, movies and/or digital videos for entertainment. Movies are universally liked by all 11; however, the platform on which they watch entertainment varies from mom or dad's cell phone or tablet to a big screen TV or movie theater.

Advertisers will be happy to know that when asked where they hear about new products or cool things to do, most of them said it is from commercials, which they hear on the radio in the car, or see on "TV" (again, this could be digital video or traditional television). It is good to know that ads still work, because the habits that these kids have today are going to be their preferences in the future.

Four of the 11 children said they attend religious services with their parents or grandparents. Three said they attend occasionally or on major holidays, while one said she goes regularly and likes talking to God. When asked if it is important for their friends to have the same religious and/or spiritual beliefs, all of them said it is not important to have the same beliefs as their friends.

Ten of the 11 children said they want to have families of their own. When asked at what age they think they might get married or find a partner and have children, four of them said they will be over 30 when they get married, four think they will be under 30, and three said they do not know.

When asked if they think they would attend college, eight of the 11 children said they plan to attend college. For the follow-up question about what they want to be when they grow up, 10 of the 11 listed jobs that will require them to attend college or a trade school, such as being an astronaut, teacher, coder, and a "businessman," as well three who want to be professional athletes in football, baseball and basketball.

As a follow up, I asked if they think there are jobs that boys can do that girls cannot and vice versa. Two of the boys, who said they want to be pro-athletes when they grow up, indicated that girls could not play football or baseball on the boys' teams, which received significant pushback from the girls. Eight of the 11 children said they think boys and girls can all do the same jobs. One decided not to answer.

It is impossible to understand consumer habits and the value of money at their age, but I asked anyway. Six of the 11 children identified as savers, who like to put their allowance and birthday money in a piggy bank. Five of the 11 kids said they like to spend it all immediately. This obviously does not tell us anything about the investing preferences of Generation Alpha, but it elicited laughs from all of the parents in the room.

I asked the children for their thoughts about the planet earth and what they know about the environment. Only six of the 11 children answered, but all six said that it is very important to recycle, reuse things when we can and "clean up after yourself everywhere." I do not think that last answer indicates that she is aware of her carbon footprint, but it could be an indication that she is headed there as a teen!

Finally, I asked the children if there is an issue that they think is important enough that they would write to the President of the United States or a local politician. Three of the 11 had strong opinions about what they would say in a letter. Following are their answers:

"You should tell everybody to stop polluting."

"You should tell everyone not to fight each other."

"People should stop saying mean things to each other."

As someone who has conducted research in both academic and business settings, the methods used for recruiting the focus group, for data collection and for data assessment are all credible. However, being completely honest, the validity of the findings is highly circumspect. The reality is that a group of 6-to-8-year-olds answering questions in front of their parents in a room full of peers, whom they have never met, is a big limitation that affects the validity of the findings. The good news is that in a few short years, Generation Alpha will be entering their teens and we will be hearing a lot more about them!

CHAPTER 10 | THERE IS A SOLUTION: STEPS YOU CAN TAKE TO ADJUST TO THE CHANGE

Prior to Millennials entering the workforce in the early 2000s, U.S. companies focused on pay, pensions and benefits as the primary means of attracting talented workers. Millennials changed that. As I have stated, we raised them to value work-life balance, being with friends and family over being workaholics, and loving what they do versus working themselves to death to earn money.

When this large group of young adults entered the job market, companies were forced to focus on dramatically shifting how they view employee benefit programs. Thanks to Millennials, we have seen innovative employee programs: employee resource groups to further personal and career development; paternity leave that men actually take to share in caring for their newborn children; a shift from company matches for 401ks to company matches for student loan payments; and perks that make working long, stressful hours more palatable, like yoga classes at lunch and healthy, free snacks (admittedly, those two also tend to keep people at their desks later in the day).

In 2015, we started to see the effects of Gen Z entering the corporate world and it is clear that their expectations expand on those that were introduced by the Millennials. The overall theme for both Millennials and Gen Z is workplace well-being. Experts writing for the *Harvard Business Review* examined why positive work cultures are more productive and stated that in today's world, "Employees prefer workplace wellbeing [sic] to material benefits."[155]

Workplace well-being is not only about standing desks, gym memberships and mid-day meditation. It is about quality of life. Good air quality and feeling comfortable (not too cold or too hot); access to natural lighting, instead of fluorescent lighting; and the ability to personalize their workspace.[156]

In a 2019 study of 1,600 workers, 66.7 percent of respondents said they would go to or stay at a company that was focused on their health and well-being.[157] That is the bottom line and it directly affects an organization's bottom line. Workplace well-being, not money, is what makes people more productive, and it is not just the Millennial workers who say that.

Why do I say that workplace well-being affects the bottom line? Employees who are happy at work are 16 percent more productive and 18 percent more likely to stay at their jobs or at their current company.[158] Let us also review a few statistics about unhappy workers, lost productivity and the other side of the real costs to your company's bottom line that were mentioned way back at the beginning of the book!

- Employee stress is a massive drain on revenue. One estimate claims that worker stress can cost American companies between $200 to $300 billion per year. That number includes issues like absenteeism, job turnover, workers' compensation claims, health issues due to stress and more.[159]

- Speaking of job turnover, it costs an average of 1.5 times an employee's salary to replace that person when you include the cost of recruiting, onboarding and training, plus the lost productivity that goes with bringing a new hire up to speed. For more junior workers, those costs are lower and for more senior positions, that cost is actually higher.[160]

- Workplace bullying, which includes verbal abuse, sabotage or work interference, and intimidating/demeaning co-workers,[161] is estimated by one source to cost $8 billion in lost productivity (there is that billion number again) and $16 million in employee turnover.[162]

- Employees who are unhappy can act out with anger and deception. Intentional fraud and theft at work cost American companies $600 billion a year in the early 2000s.[163] That does not account for the immeasurable loss in revenue from grumpy employees who mistreat your customers and vendors.

An organization is a system and, if a system is sick, it does not produce well. Think of worker unhappiness, bullying and stress like an invisible cancer that will infect your organization and destroy it from the inside out. Company managers who fall into the Baby Boomer and Silent Generation age range often still believe it is about the money. Younger workers, on the other hand, stay at companies as a life choice. Most young adults will switch jobs for a 10 percent increase and a desired perk. If the company is lucky, the younger worker might give them an opportunity to counter, but that does not always happen. In a tight labor market, such as the one that the United States was in for over 10 years after the Great Recession, that was a costly problem for companies.

Success Is as Easy as 1, 2, 3...

Below is a list of what successful companies are doing to attract and retain Millennial and Gen Z workers:

1. The overall theme for Millennials and Gen Z is that workplace well-being is more important than material benefits—but it is important that you ask your employees what they want instead of assuming that you know.

2. Engage your younger employees by providing meaningful opportunities to work on key projects.

3. Provide workplace mobility, because Millennials will stay at a job longer if they know there is opportunity for professional and personal growth.

4. Groom junior workers for leadership positions by giving them oversight of projects, budgets and other employees.

5   The annual review is a relic of the past, because younger workers want relevant and substantive feedback regularly. Consistent informal feedback is key with formal reviews given two to four times per year.

6   A flexible work environment is vital. Whether it is vacation time, parental leave or working from home, these younger generations demand a saner way to work. This policy is good for everybody, especially shareholders. People are more productive at work when they are able to focus on their jobs and not stress about showing up for their personal lives.

7   Offer a variety of employee incentive programs, because today's workers feel more cared for by companies that recognize a job well done when it happens with spot bonuses or tickets to cool events.

8   If your company only just embraced the open-office floor design, it is already time to rethink it. Independent and self-motivated Gen Zers seem to prefer their own, private space.

9   Have the most updated technological systems if you want to attract Gen Z workers.

10 Transparency about what is happening at your company is key, so communicate with Gen Z clearly and often.

11 Reverse mentoring—pairing young employees with older executives to teach the senior executives about technology and trends—is a good program that helps the business and also engages younger employees in a way that makes them feel valued at work.

12 A positive corporate culture is essential. Gen Z wants a supportive work environment with good relationships.

13 Workplace well-being is fundamental, but Gen Z has a "show me the money" attitude, because they are well informed about what jobs pay thanks to websites that track salary ranges at companies.

14 Promote diversity and inclusion for Gen Z—the most diverse population ever in the U.S. comprising 50-percent Caucasian and 50-percent other ethnicities.

15 Take a stand, because it is good for business. Your organization needs to have a point of view on social and political issues, and you need to back it up with actions, not just words.

What Millennials Need at Work

I think it is helpful to look at the above list in more detail. In order to talk about what companies need to do to successfully recruit and retain young workers, it is important to separate these two generations, because their interests are similar, but not identical. Let us first look at ways that companies successfully involve their Millennial staffers.

Millennials need to be meaningfully engaged. What does that mean? Young people have a lot of distractions today that go far beyond the concerns of 30-year-olds in the 1970s and 80s. A Gallup report stated that 55 percent of Millennials are disengaged at work.[164] The majority of Millennials are highly educated and they like being in the center of the action. It is important to realize that today's young adults are entering the workforce with more training and practical work experience than any generation before them. Entrust them with responsibilities on key projects and invite them to participate in presentations to senior management or the client. This is especially key for younger Millennials who are in their mid-twenties to early thirties and tend to occupy more junior positions.

Help them move up—or across—the corporate ladder more

quickly. Millennials are ambitious and they are being held back by older workers who are staying in the workforce longer and not freeing up more senior positions. Employee mobility is key, because Millennials are quick to job hop. As stated earlier, they will leave a company for a small increase and a perk, if they think it means a better opportunity for advancement. Most Millennials—90 percent—are looking to grow their careers at their current companies.[165] This is the low hanging fruit, so grab it! Remember, it costs 1.5 times an employee's salary to replace him or her.

Groom junior employees to move into management positions. Give them important responsibilities, like overseeing projects, handling budgets and managing other employees. Do not keep everything for yourself; let the Millennial employees learn and grow. They will be excited about work and your senior managers will have less to do, which frees them up to handle big picture tasks.

Believe it or not, this generation, which older workers have labeled as entitled and lazy, actually wants substantive performance feedback and more of it. That is right. They want to do well at work, and they want to get ahead—which is hard to do when you have 65-year-old-plus workers who are not retiring, thereby making it harder to move up the corporate ladder!

I think part of the reason Millennials have been labeled as entitled and lazy is because of their demand for flex time. It is vital to Millennials (and now Gen Z) to have flexibility. Think: generous vacation time and parental leave—for both moms and dads, as well as working remotely and coming in late or leaving early for exercise classes, taking a dog to the vet or attending a child's recital. These younger generations live on their smartphones—so physically being in the office at specific times is not as vital as it once was.

Update your incentive programs. It is not about the money, but Millennials also will not stay at a job because they get cool outdoor gear after 10 years and a gold watch after 25. Try different rewards offered more regularly, such as great seats at a sporting event and spot bonuses ($100 at the boss's discretion, because an employee went the extra mile on a project last week). Even Gen X can get on board with this. Some workers may still want the gold watch, but the younger generations would prefer some type of smartwatch.

What Gen Z Needs at Work

In looking at what the new Gen Z employees want so far from their ideal company, it is fair to say that they are on board with almost everything that the Millennial workers are demanding, plus more. We will start with where the two generations seem to differ.

A recent trend in corporate America has been open offices to foster the group-think workstyle of Millennials. Get ready for a redesign, or at least a tweak, because Gen Zers would rather have their own space.[166] Raised by their Gen X parents to be independent and self-motivated, Gen Z is not as enamored with the collaborative environment championed by Millennials.

Both generations embrace digital communications. Information for Gen Z is key, and email is for dinosaurs. So, your company's internal communications systems and processes need to be modern. And by modern, I mean, the latest software that is accessible from a mobile phone. A whopping 91 percent of Gen Zers want to work with sophisticated technology.[167]

Make sure to use your state-of-the-art tech to communicate with Gen Z clearly and often. As the first fully digital generation, Gen Z grew up with information at their fingertips, so they expect transparency from their employers. There is an old adage about managing a boss that applies here: No surprises! If your company is going through a hard time or there are rumors that you are going to be acquired or shut down, hold town hall meetings, live online chats and open forums where employees can ask the CEO anything. Companies like Apple, Facebook and Condé Nast engage in these types of practices and are able to retain young workers because of it. Be as upfront as you can within legal limits about what is going on and what may or may not happen. If your

Gen Z—and Millennial—employees hear it from you, they are more likely to believe the company and carry the message than believe the outside rumors.

When I worked at Condé Nast, the majority of the employees were Millennials and Gen Z. I mentioned in an earlier chapter that as the head of communications for the entertainment division, I was one of the five oldest people in a division of more than 300 employees, and I was not even 50 years old. Condé Nast understands its Millennial and Gen Z workers. The company is very good at being transparent, communicating with its workforce and giving younger employees a lot of responsibility for fast-paced professional growth.

At Condé Nast, we held open Q&As with our CEO on Slack, which was the primary form of internal communication at the company. Keep in mind that your full name and photo identify you on Slack, so there is no hiding behind an anonymous social media handle. Regardless, our young adult staff were never bashful about telling our CEO at the time, Bob Sauerberg, exactly what they thought and what they needed.

As a senior executive, I often watched our "Ask Bob Anything" sessions on Slack while biting off half of my nails. Our young staff was not shy about what they said to Bob and, no matter what Bob was asked, he answered openly and honestly. A few questions that stand out for me are:

> "Why can't we have an inexpensive gym, instead of one that only the senior executives can afford?"

> "Why don't we have transgender bathrooms?"

> "When will the U.S. office be reviewing salaries to ensure men and women are paid the same?" (Our UK counterparts had recently been government mandated to publish a report illuminating the disparity between male and female salaries.)

Transparency and two-way communication are tantamount, but they are not everything. Companies that understand and respect the needs of young adults are willing to take more risks so that their employees can grow professionally and move up the corporate ladder. A prime example is Elaine Welteroth, who became the youngest editor-in-chief in Condé Nast's history at age 29 when she took the reins of *Teen Vogue*.

Another example is the annual Hackathon hosted by my division, Condé Nast Entertainment. Every year, we presented our employees with a business challenge with which the Senior Staff had been grappling. The employees were assigned to teams that had a good cross section of skill sets and given 36 hours to come up with an innovative solution. The winning team won prize money, recognition in front of the entire company and an opportunity to help implement the new idea.

Along these same lines, reverse mentoring is a smart program that benefits both younger and older workers, and it speaks directly to the Gen Z and Millennial need to be valued and respected at work. Companies like The Hartford, Target, Microsoft, United Health and GE (as far back as 20 years ago) have all used reverse mentoring programs to improve business operations and employee development. Reverse mentoring is not just good for business, it is good for developing corporate culture and retaining employees. Financial services company Pershing noted a 96 percent retention rate among the young employees involved in its reverse mentoring program![168]

As mentioned, workplace well-being is more important than material benefits to most of today's workers, so it is not a surprise that corporate culture is vital to Gen Z. They want supportive leaders and good relationships at work.[169] This means that a toxic corporate culture with mercurial bosses and backstabbing colleagues will likely drive away talented Gen Z workers.

Please do not assume that workplace well-being means that money is not important. Gen Z expects you to show them the money. More so than Millennials, who entered the workforce just before the Great Recession and suffered financially because of it. Gen Z is being taught that they bring value to the jobs they do, and they expect their worth to be reflected in their salaries. However, in my experience, they are also pragmatic. I have had negotiations with Gen Z staffers where I have explained why the salary is what it is and why I cannot go higher, and they have accepted that, taken the job and stayed in it for more than the current two-year norm.

As mentioned earlier, Gen Z comprises 50 percent Caucasian and 50 percent other ethnicities,[170] so diversity and equality are vital. Companies that are successful with this generational co-hort must honor inclusion. That means the workforce needs to be diverse, salaries need to be equitable, and benefits and employee programs need to recognize and appreciate the different ethnic, racial, religious, sexual and gender practices.

Finally, let us look at one of the biggest changes I think we have ever seen in corporate America. In a complete shift from practices of the past, it is vital to Gen Zers—as consumers and as employees—that your organization has a point of view on social and political issues. These young workers want to know what you stand for and they want to see you back that up with actions, not just words.

An example of this is Chick-fil-A and Nike, which was men-tioned earlier in the book. These are two companies on opposite ends of the political spectrum, yet popular with teens, according to a bi-annual survey of teen brand popularity by Piper Jaffray & Co.[171] In that same survey, Ariana Grande and Donald Trump are the number one and two most popular celebrities, respectively.[172] You cannot get any more outspoken, or politically opposite, than Grande and Trump.

Similarly, Walmart and Sephora are among the top "Beauty Destinations." Walmart has conservative roots in Bentonville, Arkansas, but the company has made major changes in recent years to help attract and retain young workers and consumers. Among those are Walmart's political advocacy for LGBTQ rights[173] and its change on gun sales policies after a spate of mass shootings, including one that occurred in its own store in Texas.[174]

The point being that corporations have to walk the talk. It is not enough to say you stand for something; today's companies need to actually stand for that thing—liberal or conservative, Republican or Democrat, pro-this or anti-that.

All of this ties into what was discussed in the previous chapter, because everything above can be distilled into four overarching themes that are tantamount to recruiting and retaining young adults for your workforce:

1   Management should understand and respect the needs of their young adult workforce.

2   Management should be transparent and communicate with employees.

3   Management should ask employees what they need and listen to what they have to say.

4   The company's processes for raises, promotions and opportunities for professional growth are equal, fair and clear.

It Isn't a Fad; Some of These Changes Are Permanent

Starting in 2009, the United States began a period of unparalleled economic growth. When profit is good, companies have more money and resources to invest in employees and corporate culture. They spend on perks and employee programs. When there is an economic contraction—i.e., a recession—those perks and programs go away. Employees become less of a focus, as the company concentrates on shoring up their core business, while lowering costs, which often includes laying off workers.

Additionally, a booming economy in the U.S. for over 10 years created a tight labor market. In 2018 and 2019, it was really hard to attract and retain good workers. Companies went to extraordinary measures to differentiate themselves with perks and employee friendly policies—flex hours, generous family leave policies, employee advancement and training programs, snacks, company subsidized cafeterias, dry cleaning services, free shuttles to work, cash back for riding your bike to the office, and more.

As of the writing of this book in early 2020, it is yet to be determined if any of that will change in an economic downturn. One thing, however, can be said for certain—companies that squeeze out profits by eliminating employee friendly programs will not survive with Millennials and Gen Z. This change is not about money; it is about the collective values of two generations who will not tolerate business as usual. Work-life balance, respect, professional growth and corporate transparency are not going away just because money gets tight. Not with these two generations.

CHAPTER 11 | THE DEFINITIVE SOLUTION

The definitive solution is one that is familiar to all Americans and is just two words: due process.

One of the most important ways that organizations—and individuals—can deal with the changes being brought by Millennials and Gen Z is through due process. Making sure EVERYBODY is heard. Not just the ones complaining the loudest about the most sensitive problems.

It is exciting that the United States is waking up to the diverse needs of Americans. With social media, people have a voice that they never had before, and we are listening to each other in ways that we have never done. Sexual harassment and abuse, government corruption, unfair labor practices, equal pay and racism are all being exposed and discussed as they never have been.

Gen Z and Millennials are defining what society pays attention to, because power is no longer top down. It used to be that politicians, celebrities and industry leaders, who had access to newspaper reporters and television news, defined the flow of information and the power hierarchy in the United States.

Today, the power is in the hands of "a self-organizing online flash mob."[175] That quote sounds negative, but it does not have to be. The shift in power started with Occupy Wall Street in 2011 to protest economic inequality, strengthened in 2017 with the birth of the #MeToo movement, and progressed with the Hong Kong protests against the Chinese government in the summer of 2019.

Thanks to social media, communication is peer-to-peer. However, we are lacking due process. Social media enables us to serve as prosecutor, judge and jury. When something happens on social media—in the public eye—corporate and government leaders make snap decisions in minutes or hours without giving the appropriate time and space for the defendant to be heard.

This practice is now translating to how we conduct ourselves in day-to-day business. As companies develop no tolerance policies, workers who make honest mistakes, or have their actions misinterpreted by an accuser, are reprimanded quickly without adequate due process. We have become a society that is quick to judge circumstantial evidence and react, as opposed to taking an impartial stance and gathering the facts.

Intolerance met by intolerance only leads to more intolerance. When we blame and shame, people become defensive and locked into their own belief systems. In those cases, in which someone has done something that a company (or society) deems immoral and unethical, we lose the teaching moment and the opportunity for that person to change when we accuse, humiliate and punish. This axiom is true of big public messes, as well as small private ones in the workplace.

I suspect that some people reading this may think that I am saying we should treat bad actors gently. I want to make sure I am being clear—people need to be held accountable for their actions. Victims have the right to be heard and believed. Negative interactions (such as bullying and sexual harassment) that are harmful to someone's personal safety and professional well-being need to be taken seriously and addressed by organizations.

What I am talking about is how it happens to ensure that the results are fair and that the person being accused of creating a hostile work environment can learn from the experience instead of becoming embittered by it.

I am going to outline a few examples that demonstrate what I am saying.

ABC canceled its hit series *Roseanne* within hours of its

eponymous star sending a racially charged tweet in the middle of the night. Where is the due process in that? Emotions, not logic, ruled that decision and the result was anger on all sides. A *Washington Post* story a year after the tweeting incident indicated that Barr and her family firmly believe that she was fired for her political beliefs.[176] It does not take a psychologist to realize that there is no change in understanding on either side. I believe this situation represents a lost opportunity to up level the conversation around racism, as well as around freedom of speech and the responsibility that comes with it.

In 2017, as the #MeToo movement was igniting after explosive allegations against multiple Hollywood power players, another well-known Hollywood insider, documentary filmmaker Morgan Spurlock, wrote his own essay outing himself as being part of the problem. Spurlock wrote an introspective piece, which he posted on social media, exposing his own chauvinistic and harassing behavior—behavior that at one time seemed acceptable in an industry that coined the decades-old term "the casting couch" (a euphemism for the sexual abuse and harassment that women and men sometimes undergo in order to get acting jobs in the entertainment industry).

Two years later, in 2019, Spurlock conducted an in-depth Q&A with reporter Mike Fleming Jr of *Deadline Hollywood* about the incident and trying to rebuild his life and career.[177] Spurlock again expressed remorse for his behavior—but he had already done that in his essay in 2017. The surprise revelation in the interview was the speed with which all of the projects that Spurlock was involved with were abandoned by networks and film studios, and all of the people who lost their jobs as a result. This was a man who admitted fault and was trying to understand and explain his bad behavior.

Did everyone involved learn from this? Yes, they did. What did they learn? Among other things, never admit fault in public, lest you end up with a self-inflicted wound that costs you, your family, friends and colleagues their livelihoods.

Similarly, Al Franken—whom I mentioned in Chapter 6—

attempted a public comeback in 2019, two years after he resigned from the Senate amidst accusations by a female reporter that he inappropriate groped and kissed her a decade earlier. In July 2019, Franken told *The New Yorker* that he "absolutely" regretted resigning and wished that he had instead appeared in front of the Senate Ethics Committee, as he had originally requested before being pressured by Senate colleagues to resign.[178]

What did Franken learn? I am sure he learned that women have felt subjugated and abused for centuries and we finally have a voice and a platform on which to express that. But he also learned that he bowed to peer pressure instead of standing up for himself and allowing DUE PROCESS to adjudicate the situation. He told *The New Yorker*, "In my heart, I've not felt right about it." Other Senate colleagues expressed a similar sentiment in The New Yorker story when asked about pressuring Franken to quit instead of allowing the Senate Ethics Committee to investigate the charges.

Finally, in late 2019, CBS's popular series *Survivor* dealt with its first ever case of sexual harassment during the filming of the game. Contestant Kellee Kim accused fellow contestant Dan Spilo of unwanted touching. The incidents with Kim and Spilo on *Survivor* gave us a very public look at something that happens in the workplace regularly. To be clear, the filming of a TV series is a workplace setting, albeit not one in an office.

It is difficult, if not impossible, for companies to manage workplace hostilities in a way that will make the accuser and the accused feel positively about the experience. What is key to all of these situations is the following: Was it handled fairly and in a way that the victim was taken seriously, and the accused had an opportunity to defend himself or herself?

It would appear as though *Survivor* and CBS tried to do just that. Kim told Spilo to stop touching her and she expressed to producers—on camera—that it made her feel uncomfortable. The producers talked to Spilo, told him to stop and issued a warning that any continued unwanted touching on his part would result in his being ousted from the show. Spilo apologized and said it was not his intention to make anyone feel uncomfortable. This seemed like a fair and appropriate response to the accusations.

The problem became that Spilo was apparently unable to contain his tendencies and was again accused of inappropriate touching in an incident that happened off camera with a female crew member.[179] Spilo was ejected from the show and Kim later said that she was angry and hurt, because she "was not heard or believed."[180] *Survivor* host Jeff Probst said in the season finale that the show could have handled it better and they have changed the rules of the game to address issues like this in the future.

From outward appearances, this incident was handled in a way that the victim's accusations were finally understood. The accused was given an opportunity to defend himself and change his behavior, which he was not able to do. The result was that he was let go from the show (in other words, he was fired). As of the writing of this book, it is too soon to know if Spilo can see how his actions made the women feel uncomfortable. He apologized, but we do not yet know what he learned or if the situation will result in a positive change for Spilo moving forward.

Since we have been looking at a lot of cases that involve sexual assault and harassment, let us stay with that theme and explore the polarizing hearing in which psychology professor Christine Blasey Ford and Supreme Court nominee Brett Kavanaugh both testified in front of the Senate Judiciary Committee in 2018 about Kavanaugh's alleged sexual attack of Blasey Ford when they were at a party in high school. Both Blasey Ford and Kavanaugh were adamant about their respective truths. Blasey Ford took and passed a lie-detector test about the incident. Kavanaugh denied that he was ever at such a party or that the sexual assault occurred. The witness named also could not corroborate the story. Blasey Ford was publicly supported by liberals and viciously maligned by conservatives. Kavanaugh was confirmed to the Supreme Court days after the hearing.

That is due process. Both parties were given an opportunity to give a statement, provide proof and answer questions about the incident. Both held firm to their truths and there was no evidence that could adequately support either truth (polygraph tests—which are easily manipulated because they measure biological responses and not the actual telling of the truth or lying—are mostly inadmissible in court).[181]

In an earlier chapter, I discussed the fight or flight response. I mentioned studies that have been done with witnesses to a crime or accident in which their recollections of the events vary dramatically. They are not lying in telling their version of what they saw. They processed the information differently and so remember it differently. I also mentioned the power of the amygdala, the small part of our limbic brain that dictates how big our emotional response is to an event. Let me take this one step further and use a personal example.

In high school, I was with a friend in Martha's Vineyard during the summer. We were doing what a lot of precocious 16-year-old girls do—we were hanging out with older men. Some were in college, but the one that I ended up connecting with was 10 years older than me. We went into a bedroom to fool around. I thought we were just kissing, but he assumed it was more involved. Having very little sexual experience at that point, I did not know the difference between someone kissing me and someone who thought he was going to have sex. As a certain point, he said to me, "Either blow me or fuck me, your choice."

In that moment, I was terrified and frozen. I did not know what to do. I did not have the experience, courage, strength, fortitude, ability (insert whatever word you want here) to say, "No!" Instead, I chose what I considered to be the lesser of two evils, because I did not want to have unprotected sex. I also never told my girlfriend, because I was ashamed of doing something that I thought was slutty and I was embarrassed that I did not have the confidence to say no to him.

I have never forgotten that moment and I have subsequently been told by a therapist that it was rape. At the time, I did not see it as rape—and I guarantee you that he did not either. I thought I had put myself in a grown-up situation and I had to deal with what happened to me as a result.

However, the incident left an indelible mark on my memory, because my amygdala registered it as a huge emotional event. If I took a polygraph test about it today, I would pass with flying colors. I have not seen him since, so I am certain that, if he were confronted about it today, he would not remember me or the sexual encounter. For him, it was just another one-night stand. It did not register with his amygdala and the memory is long gone from his mind, because he has no idea anything went wrong. If we both had to stand in front of a court and talk about the incident, we would both be telling the truth.

Putting aside our opinions about the Blasey Ford and Kavanaugh Senate hearing and whether or not justice was served, there are plenty of other reasons for us, as Americans, to say that due process does not always work. Innocent people go to jail. Guilty people go free. It happens all the time. Sometimes the facts are corrected and someone is exonerated, but often they are not.

Due process is a system that America's founders developed that stems from British law. In fact, it goes back to the Magna Carta, which was a charter of rights signed by King John of England in the year 1215. Chapter 39 of the Magna Carta states, "[n]o free man shall be taken or imprisoned or disseized or exiled or in any way destroyed, nor will we go upon him nor send upon him, except by the lawful judgment of his peers or by the law of the land."[182]

This is the basis for due process—that no free man will be "exiled or in any way destroyed ... except by the lawful judgment of his peers or by the law of the land." Okay, let us unpack that for a moment. What is "the lawful judgement of his peers" in the modern era?

Today, lives and livelihoods are destroyed in minutes, because we are quick to assume the worst, pass judgement, and react with anger and vitriol on social media. Yes, social media has given the public a voice that we did not previously have. And thanks to the internet with its multitudinous chat groups, blogs and websites dedicated to every topic under the sun, there are no longer gatekeepers to freedom of expression. We no longer have to rely on newspapers, TV news, radio shows, celebrities or politicians to be heard. We can do it peer-to-peer on the internet and on social media, for everyone in the world to witness.

BUT this unencumbered freedom comes with great responsibility, which I would argue many of us are not exercising. At this point, I am not talking about America's legal due-diligence process, I am talking about our emotional intelligence and social interactions.

One of my oldest and dearest friends has daughters in elementary school in New York. I was over for dinner one night as the girls were discussing the social skills they are being taught by their school called the RULER curriculum, which was developed at Yale University.[183] The five pillars of RULER outlined below are the emotional version of what I am talking about when I say we need to reintroduce due process into our personal and professional interactions.

What follows is my take on RULER, which focuses on pausing during a conversation or heated situation and thinking about what is happening for both parties. It takes self-awareness and empathy to do this, but it is a valuable approach. (If you want to know more from them directly, visit their website at www.rulerapproach.org.)

"Recognizing emotions in oneself and others"

This is the first time we are encouraged to pause and think: What is happening here? Are we acting from emotion or logic? Am I or is the other person being emotionally sensitive?

"Understanding the causes and consequences of emotions"

Again, pause and think for a moment: What caused me to feel this way and what will happen if I yell, say something shaming, or do something mean and spiteful?

"Labeling emotions with a nuanced vocabulary"

In that paused moment, ask yourself: Am I feeling angry, sad, embarrassed, ashamed, afraid, etc.? Why do I feel this way? Did that person say or do something to cause it?

"Expressing emotions in accordance with cultural norms and social context"

While I am in a pause, what would be the best way for me to respond here? What would benefit me in the long run and what would be helpful to the other person? Also, understanding culture is important. For example, in Italy, it is culturally acceptable to argue loudly and use your hands to gesticulate. However, in Japan that would not be appropriate, because the cultural practice is to avoid giving a negative response, even if someone disagrees with you.

"Regulating emotions with helpful strategies"

I will give you an example of a helpful strategy, but you are welcome to come up with one of your own. Or Google it. There are plenty of self-help/life hacks online.

From 2008 until 2012, I was in school getting a master's in clinical psychology and then a doctorate in transpersonal psychology. As part of attaining those two degrees, I worked as a therapist trainee and then as a life coach teaching people to recognize conditioned thinking, clear old patterns, and achieve higher levels of personal and professional success. To help people get control of hurtful thoughts and behaviors, I created a helpful strategy called the Core-SELF Method.

The word SELF in Core-SELF is an acronym. It stands for the following:

Stop > Evaluate > Love the voice > Frame it differently

The steps are to **first** stop what you are doing, so you can catch the negative thinking.

Second, you evaluate the thinking and ask, "Why am I thinking this and is it really, really true?"

Third, approach it from a loving perspective by speaking kindly to the negative voice in your head that is telling you that your life is going to hell and you are the worst person in the world.

Fourth, frame it differently by looking at the thought from a different perspective. Sometimes this requires asking a friend, family member or colleague to give you that perspective.

Einstein famously said that the level of mind that created the problem is not the same level of mind that is going to fix it. We have to up level our thinking, which will in turn up level our behavior. And just so you do not think I am sitting here in judgement, I am on the top of the list of people who needs to practice this more.

I was born and raised in New York City, but I lived in Los Angeles for 30 years. I used to tell my LA friends, "I can go from nice to New Yorker in a heartbeat." All of my friends know that means I can go from being a kind and tolerant person to a raving lunatic in a split second. I am back living in New York and, if I am having a bad day, I am the first one to blurt out an expletive-laden crack if a stranger does something that I think is unfair or unjust—especially if it is on the subway during rush hour.

The changes I am talking about to up level our emotional-social interactions are about progress, not perfection. Imagine this scenario in business or on Twitter: Instead of reacting from defensiveness and anger while wagging our finger, what if we examine the other person's belief systems and our own belief systems?

What if we ask the other person why they believe what they believe instead of attacking them for believing it?

Instead of acting impulsively and assuming the worst in people, what if we assume the best?

What if we allow both sides to speak and to be heard?

What if the woke policies that now permeate business and academia are allowed to stay, but we let go of the rigid no-tolerance policies that do not allow for people to be human, make mistakes and learn from those mistakes?

There is a parable that I was taught several years ago that may seem overly earnest, but if I have not tipped the sappy scale yet with what I wrote above, then this teaching could resonate with you. I include it here as food for thought. My hope is for us to work together as a country to up level our interactions in order to keep the U.S. on the cutting edge of change and innovation—up leveling business and society as a whole.

If you want to change the world, start with your country.

If you want to change your country, start with your state.

If you want to change your state, start with your city.

If you want to change your city, start with your neighborhood.

If you want to change your neighborhood, start with your block.

If you want to change your block, start with your house.

If you want to change your house, start with you.

JOANNA'S BIOGRAPHY | The Short Story Version

I grew up in the entertainment industry. As a kid and teen living in New York City, I worked in front of the camera as a commercial actress and model.

I thought acting and modeling were boring. Keep in mind that this was before cell phones and the internet as we know it, so when I was on set, there was nothing to do but watch everyone work until the director or photographer started shooting.

As an actress and model, I was always more interested in what everyone was doing behind the camera. They looked like they were busy, and their minds were occupied. I was just sitting there idly waiting for someone to call action while other people tinkered with lights, camera aperture, sound and set design.

I thought a career behind the camera would be more interesting. I quit acting and moved to Los Angeles after high school to attend the University of Southern California (USC).

I am possibly the only person in the world who moved to LA to quit acting.

At USC, I did not know what I wanted to do, but I knew I wanted to be a business executive. My mom was one of the first female financial advisors on Wall Street in the 1960s and my father was one of the Mad Men of Madison Avenue, so my primary role models were executives who worked in insanely stressful and tough industries. It is fitting that I ended up working as an executive in Hollywood—an insanely stressful and tough industry.

In college, I studied journalism with an emphasis in PR and started working at an international PR agency after I graduated. My clients included food and beverage companies, such as Nestlé (our Christmas gifts were 10-pound chocolate bars that were 3 feet long!) and travel and tourism businesses, like the MGM Grand Resort & Casino in Las Vegas, which was the largest hotel in the world when we opened it in 1994. It was a good starter job and I learned a lot.

My second job out of college was as a publicist for the CBS Television Network. That kicked off a long career behind the camera in Hollywood. I spent a few years publicizing TV shows and working with CBS stars like Chuck Norris, Dudley Moore, Harvey Fierstein, Nancy McKeon, Mariska Hargitay, Michele Lee, Joan Van Ark, John Amos, Meredith Baxter, Harry Anderson, and Shadoe Stevens to name a few. I arranged talk show appearances and magazine interviews for them and escorted them on red carpets at awards shows like the Emmy Awards, Grammy Awards and People's Choice Awards.

Red carpet work sounds glamorous, and it can be, but it is also long hours and hard work. There are a lot of personalities in Hollywood. By personalities, I mean egos... including my own. We all contribute to the ego pie, which makes the work exciting and fun, but also stressful and exhausting.

As an aside, I have a group of girlfriends in a WhatsApp chat that we named "Wonder Women," because we are Wonder Women. Our group photo is, of course, Lynda Carter in her Wonder Woman costume.

I frequently send the Wonder Women photos when I am standing on red carpets with the message, "Somebody please remind me that my job is glamorous and people would love to be standing where I am right now... because nothing is going right and I have been yelled at five times already."

Inevitably one of them will look closely at whatever random photo

I have taken of the activity on the carpet and respond with something like, "OMG, is that Topher Grace talking to the press? I LOVE him. You're so lucky!"

At which point, I walk over to Topher, who happens to be a family friend, and ask him to say hi to my friend Anne, so I can send her the video of it. It is a nice moment that reminds me that one person's stress and anxiety (mine) is another person's exciting celebrity sighting (Anne's).

In the late 1990s, before the infamous Dot Bomb, I was working at a production company as the head of PR and marketing. We produced reality TV, which attracted younger viewers. Some of the series we developed and produced included *Guinness World Records Primetime* hosted by Cris Collinsworth and Mark Thompson, *Behind Closed Doors* with Joan Lunden and *Kids Say the Darndest Things* with Bill Cosby.

Back then, the programming was quick, easy and cheap to produce. It is not any more—*Survivor* changed all of that when it came to the U.S. in 2000.

This is the same period during which technology wunderkinds started to salivate at the possibility of putting entire TV series online. Commercial use of the internet and the availability of broadband streaming was becoming a reality.

My boss Eric Schotz tapped me to explore new business opportunities for us on the internet. We owned hundreds of hours of TV shows that we had produced, which were just sitting in our library waiting to make more money by being sold to distributors. This was a potential goldmine.

Eric gave me only one mandate: Don't lose money!

Eric's company was privately held and the money I spent was his profit, which was earmarked as college tuition for his three kids. Therefore, I could only make deals that would be profitable for us.

Well, in the late 1990s, everyone wanted to put content online, but nobody wanted to pay for it. Advertisers were not advertising there yet, and dot-com companies did not have the money to pay producers to license the shows.

It did not take a brain scientist to figure out that there was no way to earn money and plenty of ways to lose it under that scenario. Despite taking tons of meetings, we did not write a single deal and, a year later, the dot-com crash of 2000 happened. Popularly referred to as the Dot Bomb, all of the companies we had been talking with about licensing our content went out of business, because there was a lot of excitement around the internet in the early days, but not a lot of money. As usual, Wall Street had become euphoric about its shiny new toy—internet companies— and overvalued their stocks with hugely speculative prices for equities that had zero revenue.[184] That led to a phenomena known as a market bubble and, as we all know from playing with bubbles as kids, those things eventually burst, and when they do, they leave a slimy residue on everything in their immediate vicinity.

Unbeknownst to me at the time, this kicked off several decades of me riding the wave of change, as 18-to-34-year-olds from Gen X and Millennials to Gen Z and next Gen Alpha continue to challenge and reshape how we define content and where we watch it.

In April 2001, I got a life-changing job as the head of PR for UPN, one of only six free, over-the-air broadcast networks in the United States at the time. At the age of 32, I was a Senior Vice President with a corner office, two assistants, a bi-coastal staff, and a key parking space tapping bumpers with the CEO's car (which is a major confirmation of status in Hollywood).

Dean Valentine was the CEO of UPN and I reported to him as a member of his Senior Staff. I was the youngest officer at the network.

I controlled a multi-million-dollar P&L with oversight of my department's overhead and operating budget, and I managed six areas—corporate communications, entertainment publicity, broadcast publicity, the photography department, talent relations and corporate social responsibility.

Every company has a target market and UPN's demo was 18-to-34-year-olds. This is a key target demographic for advertisers, who are desperate to find ways to reach younger consumers. Since younger consumers are harder to connect with, advertisers pay more per person for those ads than they do on a television network that reaches viewers who are over 50. The simple reason is that more 50-year-olds are at home watching TV, while the 25-year-olds are out socializing with friends.

In 2001, the 18-to-34-year-olds were known as Gen X and I was in my sweet spot. These are my people, because I am a Gen Xer. I know what they like, I know how to talk with them, and I know where they go to get information, because I am one of them!

As happens with generations and Hollywood, I quickly aged out of the key demographic. Just three short years later, I still had my cool job, but my friends and I were old news, UPN had a new president and a new generation was moving into our view. UPN was owned by Viacom and, in a corporate restructuring, Leslie Moonves at CBS (also owned by Viacom at that time) took over UPN, Dean Valentine left, and Leslie brought in Dawn Ostroff.

Yes, UPN was still targeting 18-to-34-year-olds, but there was a new generation coming: Gen Y. While that name did not seem very creative, it also did not last. As we watched Gen Y come of age in the early 2000s, marketers like myself realized that what defined this generation was that they started life without the digital gadgets and toys, but as teens and young adults, they were as comfortable in a digital world as they were in the old analog one. "Millennials" became the buzzword for Gen Y—so much so that no one knows what you are talking about if you use the term Gen Y today.

At UPN, I had to find creative ways to promote shows like *America's Next Top Model*, because traditional PR methods did not work with younger audiences.

As an executive, I embrace change and love being innovative, so we arranged for one of the first online press conferences with a celebrity and bloggers. Blogging was a new thing and we were trying to find ways to incorporate these early influencers into our publicity efforts.

Tyra Banks was interviewed live by bloggers, who called in on an 800 number to ask her questions. The technological setup was awkward and rudimentary, but Tyra is the consummate pro and handled it with her signature grace and class.

We put her in a studio, pointed a camera at her and had her take questions from the bloggers on a speaker phone, which echoed feedback if the bloggers did not mute their computers after they dialed into our 800 line.

Fortunately, the technology of the times allowed us to control the footage. It is hard to imagine now, but it was not possible then for the bloggers to record the interview themselves, unless they used a camcorder, which would have produced a video image with wavy lines.

We sent video files of their interview with Tyra to each of the bloggers afterwards. It gave us complete control over the portions of the interview we wanted them to have. In other words, not the footage of Tyra yanking the earpiece out of her ear during the screeching sounds made by the audio feedback.

I also arranged the first blogger press junket on the set of *Veronica Mars*. Like I said, blogging was a new concept and the bloggers were not trained journalists. However, they were among the biggest proponents of *Veronica Mars* and they were responsible for helping the show get into the cultural zeitgeist, so I knew they were vital to our campaign.

It was a risky move. As the head of communications for a TV network, my team is responsible for managing the reputation of the network and all of our TV series. Hollywood is an insular business and the press who cover the TV and film industries have been doing it for a long time. Back then, people who were professional journalists were deemed "safe" for conducting interviews. Bloggers, who were totally unknown to us and not trained journalists, presented a risk. However, the producers and cast of *Veronica Mars* knew the fans were the key to the show's success and wanted to do it.

Blogger junkets are so standard at this point that I feel like a dinosaur saying I was the first. In fact, it was so revolutionary, the *Wall Street Journal* did a story about it that I can no longer find online. Apparently, the *Journal* also thinks the news is so outdated that it is not worthy of being archived.

After five years as the head of communications for UPN, the network was merged with its biggest rival, The WB. At that time, UPN was owned by CBS Corporation and The WB was owned by Warner Bros. After more than a decade in existence, the two networks had lost a combined $2 billion and CBS and Warner Bros. got tired of bleeding money. The two media giants decided they would be better off partnering with each other, as opposed to cannibalizing each other for similar viewers.

In 2006, they merged UPN and The WB to create a new network called The CW. My boss, Dawn Ostroff, was tapped as president of the newly formed entity. The CW launched in the fall of 2006 with the most popular programming from UPN and The WB, including reality series *America's Next Top Model*, dramas *Gilmore Girls, Smallville, Supernatural* and *Veronica Mars*, and the comedy series *Girlfriends*.

When UPN shut down, I ended up getting a job that I considered to be the best of both worlds. Nancy Tellem, who was then president of CBS Paramount Television Entertainment Group, helped bring me over to our parent company CBS as Senior Vice President of Media Relations over digital properties for the entertainment division. I also continued to work as a speech writer and consultant for The CW during its annual Advertising Upfront. (Note: The Advertising Upfront occurs every spring. The TV networks preview their fall series for the advertisers, who buy the ad time "upfront"—i.e., in advance of the series premiering in September.)

It is hard to imagine now, but in 2006, streaming online barely worked, because most people did not have enough bandwidth at home to watch a program online. Moreover, mobile phones were used to make calls and send emails and texts. Americans did not yet have the ability to watch TV on them. I single out the U.S., because certain European and Asian countries were ahead of the U.S. in mobile technology at the time, so we knew it was coming.

It was 2006 and it was a different era. The iPhone did not exist. MySpace was the most visited website, ahead of Google. YouTube was in its nascence but growing in popularity—the shaky amateur videos that looked like they belonged on an episode of *America's Funniest Home Videos* were quickly becoming the next big thing.

CBS was the first network to put some of its TV shows on-line the day after they ran on the network and I was on the front lines of making that announcement. The other networks quickly followed suit. Between my job at CBS and consulting work at The CW, I was once again on the forefront of marketing to 18-to-34-year-olds—a.k.a., Millennials.

It was an exciting time, but the economy was faltering. In addition, Hollywood was facing a writer's strike. A strike by any of the unions is a huge problem. It means TV series and feature films cannot be made, because when you remove just one piece of the creative process, the whole machine stops.

I was downsized in 2007, just before the recession. This was the second time I had been downsized in two years, since UPN was technically also a downsizing that fortunately resulted in me getting a job at CBS immediately.

Note: *My experience being downsized would not end here. Someday I will write a book about being downsized five times and managing to land on my feet each time. It is like planting a perfect 10 on the vault in a gymnastics competition. It takes years to perfect and a lot of bumps and bruises!*

I did not go back to full-time work for six years as a result of the Great Recession. Given the economy and my position as a senior executive, there were fewer job opportunities and it took longer to find a position. Since there was no chance that I was going to get work until the economy recovered in a few years, I went back to school. I studied psychology, because I have always been interested in it and I knew it would help me in business. I also worked part-time as a communications consultant. I continued as a speech writer for The CW and, for seven years, I had a front-row seat to the innovative digital extensions Dawn Ostroff and her team were experimenting with in the late-2000s.

In addition, I was hired by a friend to do some writing for a fledgling distribution platform that was streaming old TV series and movies online. It was an SVOD (streaming video on demand) provider that had success with reruns and decided it wanted to try to produce its own TV series.

This was a foreign concept at the time, because the broadcast and cable networks controlled all of the distribution channels. Basically, not many people thought an internet company could make TV shows and movies the way Hollywood could.

They were wrong. The company was Netflix.

Once again, I had a front seat to a major change that would completely disrupt the media content business. I only handled one project for Netflix—I wrote the original press kit for "House of Cards," but it was enough for me to see where the industry was headed.

Once the recession ended and I graduated from my doctoral program, I immediately went back to work in Hollywood. This time, I worked for a children's network called The Hub. It was a joint venture between Hasbro and Discovery. Our target demo was children ages 6 to 14 and families in the evenings. It was run by Margaret Loesch, a strong female CEO with an impeccable career in kids' television. It is thanks to The Hub that I first got to know Generation Z.

Gen Z was coming of age and the effects of them being our country's first all-digital generation were very clear—Netflix ruled and programming with commercials did not interest them. It also became clear that they were just as happy to watch shows on a phone and an iPad as they were to watch them on a television set.

The programming shifts threatened by digital media and on-demand viewing were no longer something on the horizon. The old way of watching TV live with commercials was quickly becoming uninteresting to millions of young viewers. The threat we had seen coming was real and the change was happening.

The Hub closed down in 2014. Kids' viewing habits had shifted dramatically and its business model did not work in the new world order. Discovery reimagined the network as Discovery Family, let go of all but a handful of employees, and ran only Hasbro-produced cartoons and repurposed programs. (Repurposed is industry jargon for programming that has first aired somewhere else.)

The problem with The Hub was that it was modeled as a full linear, cable TV channel. A few years earlier, when The Hub launched in 2010, this business model made perfect sense. In just four years, content viewing habits on digital media made it unsustainable. Netflix and YouTube played major roles in that quick and dramatic shift.

After The Hub closed, I went to Lionsgate. In 2015, Lionsgate was king of YA content. In the industry, YA stands for young adults and Lionsgate produced films like *The Hunger Games*, *The Twilight Saga* and the *Divergent* series, which targeted Millennials and Gen Z. We produced TV series and movies for Netflix, Hulu and Amazon, like the award-winning series, *Orange is the New Black* and *Casual*. We were on the forefront of developing games in VR, like the *John Wick Chronicles*. We experimented with subscription OTT (over-the-top) channels, such as Comic-Con HQ, Tribeca Shortlist and the Spanish-language movie channel, Pantaya.

The studio, which had been guided to tremendous growth by Jon Feltheimer and Michael Burns, was at the pinnacle of its success and I was working in corporate communications and housed in the C-suite. My boss, the Chief Communications Officer Peter Wilkes, is known to be an excellent wordsmith and he constructed a descriptor for the studio that we used in every press release. We used to say that Lionsgate was a "next generation global content leader," and the moniker fit. Whether it was TV, film, games or social media, Lionsgate's content was influencing two generations of entertainment junkies.

After two years at Lionsgate and decades of living in Los Angeles, I decided it was time to go home to New York City. I do not know why, after 30 years in LA, I got the bug to move home, but I was adamant that I needed to come home to NYC and the timing felt right.

While I was job hunting, I turned to my mentor and former boss Dawn Ostroff, who had moved back to New York and was president of Condé Nast Entertainment (CNE). I had worked for Dawn at two different companies at that point, but we had not worked together in several years.

My recent role at Lionsgate was very corporate with a focus on M&A and quarterly earnings. Dawn's recent experiences were all about content, especially digital video, a.k.a. short-form video. She had entered a realm about which I knew nothing, and in her wisdom as a mentor, she made sure I realized that.

We had breakfast at The Regency on the Upper East Side, and she said to me, "Joanna, you don't know anything about digital video and you're going to need to if you want to continue working in the industry." As usual, she got my attention with her frankness and her ability to get to the heart of a situation quickly.

Condé Nast Entertainment, which produces entertainment content for television, film, digital video and VR, had never had a head of communications and Dawn needed one. For my part, I had a lot of experience targeting young audiences in film, TV, games, theme parks, and OTT channels in the U.S. and abroad. I was a near perfect fit—minus the very obvious lack of knowledge about how to make a series of YouTube videos go viral and garner a few hundred million views.

Dawn made me realize that my professional experience was not keeping up with the rapid pace of change in the entertainment industry. All of my years working with digital extensions, online viewing, and OTT channels was quickly being eclipsed by short-form video, which was getting billions of views a year on You-Tube, Facebook and Snapchat.

Short-form content had also gotten the attention of the advertisers. At the time, the ad spend for short-form digital video was below that of what advertisers spend on traditional networks like CBS and Discovery, but online advertising was predicted to pass linear TV in a few years. And it did!

So, in 2017, I moved home to New York City and joined CNE as the head of communications. CNE is a B2B (business-to-business) division of publishing behemoth Condé Nast. Besides producing feature films and TV series, CNE produced and distributed more than 4,000 videos a year that garnered 12 billion views annually across 20 brands, which include *Vogue, Vanity Fair, Glamour, GQ, Bon Appétit, Wired, The New Yorker* and more.

It was a huge operation and Condé Nast was truly a next gen company. Across print, digital and social media, Condé Nast reached one-in-two Millennial females in the U.S. and one-in-three Millennial males. They were a force to be reckoned with, but not many people knew it.

At Condé Nast Entertainment, we did not do PR the way 99 percent of the country does PR. Lengthy press releases blasted out to several hundred journalists garnered NO coverage and we were promoting celebrities and zeitgeist culture. Those are the types of topics that were easy to get coverage for in the 80s, 90s and early 2000s, but not anymore.

We were not alone. PR people in business sectors across the United States were having trouble getting stories placed. A lot of my PR colleagues blamed the relentless pace of the news cycle and the unprecedented focus on politics with Donald Trump as president. But I knew it was something else.

At CNE, the members of my PR staff were in their early- to mid-twenties and we were doing what I called guerilla PR. We were using a variety of software to create highly targeted campaigns with key reporters who were going to drive views of our content.

My staff communicated with our press contacts via Twitter, Snapchat and Instagram DM (Direct Message). We spoke to reporters in a language that they related to and we A/B tested email headlines and formats by incorporating polls into our press announcements and soliciting their feedback.

The reason most of my colleagues were—and still are—having issues getting coverage is not because of political news, although that does not help. The issue is that they are using traditional PR methods to communicate with Millennial and Gen Z reporters, who think that Facebook is for old people and email was something used by dinosaurs.

Moreover, business reporters whom I had worked with for

decades would no longer write a story based on a press release that was blasted out the morning of an announcement. Everything had to be placed in advance, because the competition is too tough and the need to be first too great.

Today, PR has become a very high touch, highly targeted practice that requires in-depth knowledge of how Millennials and Gen Z receive and process information. To put it bluntly, the old way of doing PR no longer works.

My boss Dawn left CNE during the summer of 2018 to be Chief Content Officer at Spotify. Dawn is an intrapreneur (yes, that's a term). She starts new businesses inside larger corporate structures. After she has succeeded building a business, she moves on to the next challenge. So, when Dawn left, I knew it signaled my time to move to my next challenge, too.

I interviewed for a few Chief Communications Officers roles in the media industry, but nothing interested me. For years, people had been asking me when I was going to start an agency. I always thought of myself as a corporate girl. As a teen and young adult, I imagined that I would have a career at one company, work my way up the ladder and someday be CEO.

Well, that did not happen. In fact, my career has been the exact opposite. The theme of my career has been working at companies in transition in an industry marred by disruptive market forces. It is exciting, I love the work, and I have been on the front lines of significant crisis communications and employee relations issues, but it has also led me to be downsized five times.

When I was out of work during the Great Recession, I started a company in 2012 called J.D. Massey Associates, Inc., which did business as JDMA Inc. It was a corporate entity that I used for consulting work and business coaching. Over the years, I have used the company sporadically between corporate gigs.

In 2019, I was in one of my consulting phases and used the opportunity to write this book. I was consulting executives and advising companies on all facets of corporate communications with a specialty in communicating with Millennials and Gen Z as employees, consumers, investors and members of the press.

I have tremendous respect and appreciation for the changes that Millennials and Gen Z are forcing on the workplace. I love witnessing them and advising executives in the public and private sector about how to adjust to these two generations. It is a fascinating shift and I am excited to see how it continues to unfold. After all, the youngest members of Generation Z are just turning 10 years old, so we have a long way to go to see the effects of their generation on American business.

NOTES

1. Goldschein, Eric and Kim Bhasin. "14 Surprising Ways Employees Cost Their Companies Billions in the Workplace." *Business Insider*, November 29, 2011. https://www.businessinsider.com/surprising-costs-to-the-work-place-2011-11 (retrieved July 29, 2019)

2. Website. "The WBI Definition of Workplace Bullying." Workplace Bullying Institute. https://www.workplacebullying.org/individuals/problem/definition/ (retrieved July 29, 2019)

3. Goldschein, Eric and Kim Bhasin. "14 Surprising Ways Employees Cost Their Companies Billions in the Workplace." *Business Insider*, November 29, 2011. https://www.businessinsider.com/surprising-costs-to-the-work-place-2011-11 (retrieved July 29, 2019)

4. Goldschein, Eric and Kim Bhasin. "14 Surprising Ways Employees Cost Their Companies Billions in the Workplace." Business Insider, November 29, 2011. https://www.businessinsider.com/surprising-costs-to-the-work-place-2011-11 (retrieved July 29, 2019)

5. Seppälä, Emma and Kim Cameron. "Proof that Positive Work Cultures Are More Productive." Harvard Business Review, December 1, 2015. https://hbr.org/2015/12/proof-that-positive-work-cultures-are-more-productive (retrieved July 29, 2019)

6. Patel, Deep. "8 Ways Generation Z Will Differ from Millennials in the Workplace." Forbes, September 21, 2017. https://www.forbes.com/sites/deeppatel/2017/09/21/8-ways-generation-z-will-differ-from-millennials-in-the-workplace/#61476f2276e5 (retrieved June 16, 2019)

7. Giang, Vivian. "Here Are the Strengths and Weaknesses of Millennials, Gen X, and Boomers." Business Insider, September 9, 2013. https://www.businessinsider.com/how-millennials-gen-x-and-boomers-shape-the-workplace-2013-9 (retrieved May 3, 2019)

8. Dimock, Michael. "Defining Generations: Where Millennials End and Generation Z Begins." Pew Research Center, January 17, 2019. https://www.pewresearch.org/fact-tank/2019/01/17/where-millennials-end-and-generation-z-begins/ (retrieved April 30, 2019)

9. Business Insider Intelligence. "Generation Z: Latest Characteristics, Research, and Facts." and Facts." *Business Insider*, no date. https://www.businessinsider.com/generation-z (retrieved May 6, 2019)

10. Williams, Alex. "Meet Alpha: The Next 'Next Generation.'" The *New York Times*, September 19, 2015. https://www.nytimes.com/2015/09/19/fashion/meet-alpha-the-next-next-generation.html (retrieved April 18, 2019)

11. Fry, Richard, Ruth Igielnik, and Eileen Patten. "How Millennials Today Compare with their Grandparents 50 Years Ago." Pew Research Center, March 16, 2018. https://www.pewresearch.org/fact-tank/2018/03/16/how-millennials-compare-with-their-grandparents/ (retrieved June 28, 2019)

12. *Merriam-Webster*, s.v. "Generation, noun." Accessed June 16, 2019. https://www.merriam-webster.com/dictionary/generation

13. Fry, Richard. "Millennials Are the Largest Generation in the U.S. Labor Force." Pew Research Center, April 11, 2018. https://www.pewresearch.org/fact-tank/2018/04/11/millennials-largest-generation-us-labor-force/ (retrieved June 16, 2019)

14. Levin, Dan. "Generation Z: Who They Are, in Their Own Words." The *New York Times*, March 28, 2019. https://www.nytimes.com/2019/03/28/us/gen-z-in-their-words.html (retrieved June 16, 2019)

15. Fry, Richard. "Millennials Projected to Overtake Baby Boomers as America's Largest Generation." Pew Research Center, March 1, 2018. https://www.pewresearch.org/fact-tank/2018/03/01/millennials-overtake-baby-boomers/ (retrieved May 27, 2019)

16. United States Census Bureau Statistics. "U.S. and World Population Clock." United States Census Bureau, ongoing. https://www.census.gov/popclock/ (retrieved June 16, 2019 at 10:15 PM, Eastern Time)

17. Business Insider Intelligence. "Generation Z: Latest Characteristics, Research, and Facts." *Business Insider*, no date. https://www.businessinsider.com/generation-z (retrieved May 6, 2019)

18. United States Census Bureau Statistics. "U.S. and World Population Clock." United States Census Bureau, ongoing. https://www.census.gov/popclock/ (retrieved May 27, 2019 at 3:30 PM, Eastern Time)

19. Merrill Lynch Wealth Management. "Early Adulthood: The Pursuit of Financial Independence." New York: Bank of America Corporation, 2019. https://www.ml.com/early-adulthood-age-wave.html (retrieved April 23, 2019)

20. Shakespeare, William. *Romeo and Juliet*. Shakespear-online.com, 2015, Act 2, Scene 2, Lines 43–44. http://www.shakespeare-online.com/plays/romeo_2_2.html (retrieved June 17, 2019)

21. OppenheimerFunds. "Proving Worth: The Values of Affluent Millennials in North America." New York: OppenheimerFunds, December 4, 2015. http://www.campdenwealth.com/article/proving-worth---values-affluent-millennials-north-america (retrieved April 22, 2019)

22. Bromwich, Jonah. "We Asked Gen Z to Pick a Name. It Wasn't Generation Z." The *New York Times*, January 31, 2018. https://www.nytimes.com/2018/01/31/style/generation-z-name.html (retrieved June 15, 2019)

23. Bond, Shannon. "As TikTok Grows in Popularity, It's Also Setting off Alarms in Silicon Valley." NPR Technology, December 10, 2019. https://www.npr.org/2019/12/10/786835248/as-tiktok-grows-in-popularity-its-also-setting-off-alarms-in-silicon-valley (retrieved January 5, 2020)

24. Lobosco, Katie. "66% of Millennials Have Nothing Saved for Retirement." *CNN Money*, March 7, 2018. https://money.cnn.com/2018/03/07/retirement/millennial-retirement-savings/index.html (retrieved June 17, 2019)

25. Rosentiel, Tom. "Young Voters in the 2008 Election." Pew Research Center, November 13, 2008. https://www.pewresearch.org/2008/11/13/young-voters-in-the-2008-election/ (retrieved May 2, 2019)

26. Martin, Anna Sofia. "The Undetected Influence of Generation X." Forbes, September 13, 2016. https://www.forbes.com/sites/nextavenue/2016/09/13/the-undetected-influence-of-generation-x/#53830b541efb (retrieved June 17, 2019)

27. Williams, Alex. "Move Over, Millennials, Here Comes Generation Z." The *New York Times*, December 21, 2017. https://www.nytimes.com/2015/09/20/fashion/move-over-millennials-here-comes-generation-z.html (retrieved June 15, 2019)

28. American Psychological Association. "Stress in America: Generation Z." *Stress in America™ Survey*, October 2018. https://www.apa.org/news/press/releases/stress/2018/stress-gen-z.pdf (retrieved May 4, 2019)

29. Brooks, David. "Will Gen Z Save the World?" The *New York Times*, July 4, 2019. https://www.nytimes.com/2019/07/04/opinion/gen-z-boomers.html (retrieved July 14, 2019)

30. Tanzi, Alexandre. "Millennials Are Facing $1 Trillion in Debt." *Bloomberg*, February 25, 2019. https://www.bloomberg.com/news/articles/2019-02-25/millennials-face-1-trillion-debt-as-student-loans-pile-up (retrieved June 17, 2019)

31. Merrill Lynch Wealth Management. "Early Adulthood: The Pursuit of Financial Independence." New York: Bank of America Corporation, 2019. https://www.ml.com/early-adulthood-age-wave.html (retrieved April 23, 2019)

32. Merrill Lynch Wealth Management. "Early Adulthood: The Pursuit of Financial Independence." New York: Bank of America Corporation, 2019, p. 13. https://www.ml.com/early-adulthood-age-wave.html (retrieved April 23, 2019)

33. Merrill Lynch Wealth Management. "Early Adulthood: The Pursuit of Financial Independence." New York: Bank of America Corporation, 2019, p. 5. https://www.ml.com/early-adulthood-age-wave.html (retrieved April 23, 2019)

34. Merrill Lynch Wealth Management. "Early Adulthood: The Pursuit of Financial Independence." New York: Bank of America Corporation, 2019, p. 14. https://www.ml.com/early-adulthood-age-wave.html (retrieved April 23, 2019)

35. Jankowski, Paul. "Valuable Insights into the Country's Most Powerful Millennial Consumer Group." New Heartland Group, 2015, p. 4. https://newheartlandgroup.com/millennial-whitepaper/ (retrieved May 2, 2019)

36. Jankowski, Paul. "Valuable Insights into the Country's Most Powerful Millennial Consumer Group." New Heartland Group, 2015, p. 4. https://newheartlandgroup.com/millennial-whitepaper/ (retrieved May 2, 2019)

37. Jankowski, Paul. "Valuable Insights into the Country's Most Powerful Millennial Consumer Group." New Heartland Group, 2015. https://newheartlandgroup.com/millennial-whitepaper/ (retrieved May 2, 2019)

38. Stahl, Ashley. "Gen Z: What to Expect from the New Workforce." *Forbes*, September 26, 2018. https://www.forbes.com/sites/ashleystahl/2018/09/26/gen-z-what-to-expect-from-the-new-work-force/#5d5f00863e05 (retrieved June 15, 2019)

39. Sandehl, Alannah. "How Generation Z Is Shaping Today's Marketing Tactics." *Forbes*, October 30, 2018. https://www.forbes.com/sites/forbesagencycouncil/2018/10/30/how-generation-z-is-shaping-todays-marketing-tactics/#571176402bc1 (retrieved June 16, 2019)

40. Patel, Deep. "8 Ways Generation Z Will Differ from Millennials in the Workplace." *Forbes*, September 21, 2017. https://www.forbes.com/sites/deeppatel/2017/09/21/8-ways-generation-z-will-differ-from-millennials-in-the-workplace/#61476f2276e5 (retrieved June 16, 2019)

41. Martin, Anna Sofia. "The Undetected Influence of Generation X." *Forbes*, September 13, 2016. https://www.forbes.com/sites/nextavenue/2016/09/13/the-undetected-influence-of-generation-x/#53830b541efb (retrieved June 17, 2019)

42. Howe, Neil. "The Silent Generation, 'The Lucky Few' (Part 3 of 7)." *Forbes*, August 13, 2014. https://www.forbes.com/sites/neilhowe/2014/08/13/the-silent-generation-the-lucky-few-part-3-of-7/#6e4d7b792c63 (retrieved June 30, 2019)

43. Wong, Vanessa. "Here's How Millennials' Lives Were Changed by Recession 10 Years Ago." *BuzzFeed News*, September 25, 2018. https://www.buzzfeednews.com/article/venessawong/millennials-lives-changed-by-recession-2008-2018 (retrieved June 30, 2019)

44. Fry, Richard. "For First Time in Modern Era, Living with Parents Edges out Other Living Arrangements for 18- to 34-Year-Olds." Pew Research Center's Social & Demographic Trends, June 10, 2016. https://www.pewsocialtrends.org/2016/05/24/for-first-time-in-modern-era-living-with-parents-edges-out-other-living-arrangements-for-18-to-34-year-olds/ (retrieved April 18, 2019)

45. Peterson, Hayley. "Millennials Are Old News—Here's Everything You Should Know about Generation Z." *Business Insider*, June 25, 2014. https://www.businessinsider.com/generation-z-spending-habits-2014-6 (retrieved June 16, 2019)

46. Schawbel, Dan. "Millennial Branding and Randstad US Release First Worldwide Study Comparing Gen Y and Gen Z Workplace Expectations." Millennial Branding, September 2, 2014. http://millennialbranding.com/2014/geny-genz-global-workplace-expectations-study/ (retrieved June 16, 2019)

47. Patel, Deep. "8 Ways Generation Z Will Differ from Millennials in the Workplace." *Forbes*, September 21, 2017. https://www.forbes.com/sites/deeppatel/2017/09/21/8-ways-generation-z-will-differ-from-millennials-in-the-workplace/#61476f2276e5 (retrieved June 16, 2019)

48. Pew Research Center. "The Whys and Hows of Generations Research." Pew Research Center, September 3, 2015. https://www.people-press.org/2015/09/03/the-whys-and-hows-of-generations-research/ (retrieved September 28, 2019)

49. Williams, Yolanda. "The Silent Generation: Definition, Characteristics & Facts." Study.com, no date. https://study.com/academy/lesson/the-silent-generation-definition-characteristics-facts.html (retrieved September 27, 2019)

50. Pew Research Center. "The Whys and Hows of Generations Research." Pew Research Center, September 3, 2015. https://www.people-press.org/2015/09/03/the-whys-and-hows-of-generations-research/ (retrieved September 28, 2019)

51. Taylor, Paul and George Gao. "Generation X: America's Neglected 'Middle Child.'" Pew Research Center, June 5, 2014. https://www.pewresearch.org/fact-tank/2014/06/05/generation-x-americas-neglected-middle-child/ (retrieved September 28, 2019)

52. Pew Research Center. "The Whys and Hows of Generations Research." Pew Research Center, September 3, 2015. https://www.people-press.org/2015/09/03/the-whys-and-hows-of-generations-research/ (retrieved September 28, 2019)

53. Pew Research Center. "The Whys and Hows of Generations Research." Pew Research Center, September 3, 2015. https://www.people-press.org/2015/09/03/the-whys-and-hows-of-generations-research/ (retrieved September 28, 2019)

54. Pew Research Center. "The Whys and Hows of Generations Research." Pew Research Center, September 3, 2015. https://www.people-press.org/2015/09/03/the-whys-and-hows-of-generations-research/ (retrieved September 28, 2019)

55. Pew Research Center. "The Whys and Hows of Generations Research." Pew Research Center, September 3, 2015. https://www.people-press.org/2015/09/03/the-whys-and-hows-of-generations-research/ (retrieved September 28, 2019)

56. Pew Research Center. "The Whys and Hows of Generations Research." Pew Research Center, September 3, 2015. https://www.people-press.org/2015/09/03/the-whys-and-hows-of-generations-research/ (retrieved September 28, 2019)

57. Website page. "List of Current United States Senators by Age." Infogalactic, continually updating. https://infogalactic.com/info/List_of_current_United_States_Senators_by_age (retrieved January 5, 2020)

58. Shi, Audrey. "Meet the Oldest Executives in the Fortune 500." *Fortune*, June 20, 2016. https://fortune.com/2016/06/20/fortune-500-oldest-ceos/ (retrieved September 28, 2019)

59. Pew Research Center. "The Whys and Hows of Generations Research." Pew Research Center, September 3, 2015. https://www.people-press.org/2015/09/03/the-whys-and-hows-of-generations-research/ (retrieved September 28, 2019)

60. Pew Research Center. "The Whys and Hows of Generations Research." Pew Research Center, September 3, 2015. https://www.people-press.org/2015/09/03/the-whys-and-hows-of-generations-research/ (retrieved September 28, 2019)

61. Pew Research Center. "The Whys and Hows of Generations Research." Pew Research Center, September 3, 2015. https://www.people-press.org/2015/09/03/the-whys-and-hows-of-generations-research/ (retrieved September 28, 2019)

62. Pew Research Center. "The Whys and Hows of Generations Research." Pew Research Center, September 3, 2015. https://www.people-press.org/2015/09/03/the-whys-and-hows-of-generations-research/ (retrieved September 28, 2019)

63. Pew Research Center. "The Whys and Hows of Generations Research." Pew Research Center, September 3, 2015. https://www.people-press.org/2015/09/03/the-whys-and-hows-of-generations-research/ (retrieved September 28, 2019)

64. Cohn, D'Vera and Paul Taylor. "Baby Boomers Approach 65—Glumly." Pew Research Center, December 20, 2010. https://www.pewsocialtrends.org/2010/12/20/baby-boomers-approach-65-glumly/ (retrieved September 28, 2019)

65. Cohn, D'Vera and Paul Taylor. "Baby Boomers Approach 65—Glumly." Pew Research Center, December 20, 2010. https://www.pewsocialtrends.org/2010/12/20/baby-boomers-approach-65-glumly/ (retrieved September 28, 2019)

66. Fry, Richard. "Baby Boomers Are Staying in the Labor Force at Rates Not Seen in Generations for People Their Age." Pew Research Center, July 24, 2019. https://www.pewresearch.org/fact-tank/2019/07/24/baby-boomers-us-labor-force/ (retrieved September 28, 2019)

67. Cohn, D'Vera and Paul Taylor. "Baby Boomers Approach 65—Glumly." Pew Research Center, December 20, 2010. https://www.pewsocialtrends.org/2010/12/20/baby-boomers-approach-65-glumly/ (retrieved September 28, 2019)

68. Pew Research Center. "The Whys and Hows of Generations Research." Pew Research Center, September 3, 2015. https://www.people-press.org/2015/09/03/the-whys-and-hows-of-generations-research/ (retrieved September 28, 2019)

69. Taylor, Paul and George Gao. "Generation X: America's Neglected 'Middle Child.'" Pew Research Center, June 5, 2014. https://www.pewresearch.org/fact-tank/2014/06/05/generation-x-americas-neglected-middle-child/ (retrieved September 28, 2019)

70. Kagan, Julie. "Generation X." Investopedia, June 25, 2019. https://www.investopedia.com/terms/g/generation-x-genx.asp (retrieved September 28, 2019)

71. Taylor, Paul and George Gao. "Generation X: America's Neglected 'Middle Child.'" Pew Research Center, June 5, 2014. https://www.pewresearch.org/fact-tank/2014/06/05/generation-x-americas-neglected-middle-child/ (retrieved September 28, 2019)

72. Pew Research Center. "The Whys and Hows of Generations Research." Pew Research Center, September 3, 2015. https://www.people-press.org/2015/09/03/the-whys-and-hows-of-generations-research/ (retrieved September 28, 2019)

73. Pew Research Center. "The Whys and Hows of Generations Research." Pew Research Center, September 3, 2015. https://www.people-press.org/2015/09/03/the-whys-and-hows-of-generations-research/ (retrieved September 28, 2019)

74. Pew Research Center. "The Whys and Hows of Generations Research." Pew Research Center, September 3, 2015. https://www.people-press.org/2015/09/03/the-whys-and-hows-of-generations-research/ (retrieved September 28, 2019)

75. Pew Research Center. "The Whys and Hows of Generations Research." Pew Research Center, September 3, 2015. https://www.people-press.org/2015/09/03/the-whys-and-hows-of-generations-research/ (retrieved September 28, 2019)

76. Pew Research Center. "The Whys and Hows of Generations Research." Pew Research Center, September 3, 2015. https://www.people-press.org/2015/09/03/the-whys-and-hows-of-generations-research/ (retrieved September 28, 2019)

77. Merrill Lynch Wealth Management. "Early Adulthood: The Pursuit of Financial Independence." New York: Bank of America Corporation, 2019, p. 5. https://www.ml.com/early-adulthood-age-wave.html (retrieved April 23, 2019)

78. White, Justin. "Research Finds Link Between Social Media and the 'Fear of Missing Out.'" *Washington Post*, July 8, 2013. https://www.washingtonpost.com/national/health-science/research-finds-link-between-social-media-and-the-fear-of-missing-out/2013/07/08/b2cc7ddc-e287-11e2-a11e-c2ea876a8f30_story.html?utm_term=.b81b146e7160 (retrieved June 18, 2019)

79. Welch, Ashley. "Depression, Anxiety, Suicide Increase in Teens and Young Adults, Study Finds." *CBS News*, March 14, 2019. https://www.cbsnews.com/news/suicide-depression-anxiety-mental-health-issues-increase-teens-young-adults/ (retrieved June 18, 2019)

80. Lorenz, Taylor. "The Instagram Aesthetic is Over." *The Atlantic*, April 23, 2019. https://www.theatlantic.com/technology/archive/2019/04/influencers-are-abandoning-instagram-look/587803/ (retrieved April 24, 2019)

81. Seppälä, Emma and Kim Cameron. "Proof that Positive Work Cultures Are More Productive." *Harvard Business Review*, December 1, 2015. https://hbr.org/2015/12/proof-that-positive-work-cultures-are-more-productive (retrieved July 9, 2019)

82. OppenheimerFunds. "Proving Worth: The Values of Affluent Millennials in North America." New York: OppenheimerFunds, December 4, 2015. http://www.campdenwealth.com/article/proving-worth---values-affluent-millennials-north-america (retrieved April 22, 2019)

83. Singer, Peter. "Heartwarming Causes Are Nice, but Let's Give to Charity with Our Heads." *The Washington Post*, December 19, 2013. https://www.washingtonpost.com/opinions/heartwarming-causes-are-nice-but-lets-give-to-charity-with-our-heads/2013/12/19/43469ae0-6731-11e3-a0b9-249bbb34602c_story.html?noredirect=on&utm_term=.14778d03aa70 (retrieved April 22, 2019)

84. OppenheimerFunds. "Proving Worth: The Values of Affluent Millennials in North America." New York: OppenheimerFunds, December 4, 2015. http://www.campdenwealth.com/article/proving-worth---values-affluent-millennials-north-america (retrieved April 22, 2019)

85. OppenheimerFunds. "The Generations Project." New York: OppenheimerFunds, June 12, 2018. https://www.prnewswire.com/news-releases/oppenheimerfunds-announces-new-multi-generational-high-net-worth-research-report-the-generations-project-300664896.html (retrieved April 22, 2019)

86. Harvard University, Harvard Kennedy School. "Spring 2019 Harvard IOP Youth Poll Results." *Harvard Institute of Politics*, Spring 2019. https://iop.harvard.edu/about/newsletter-press-release/spring-2019-harvard-iop-youth-poll-results (retrieved May 6, 2019)

87. Harvard University, Harvard Kennedy School. "Spring 2019 Harvard IOP Youth Poll Results." *Harvard Institute of Politics*, Spring 2019. https://iop.harvard.edu/about/newsletter-press-release/spring-2019-harvard-iop-youth-poll-results (retrieved May 6, 2019)

88. Parker, Kim, Nikki Graf, and Ruth Igielnik. "Generation Z Looks a Lot Like Millennials on Key Social and Political Issues." Pew Research Center, January 17, 2019. https://www.pewsocialtrends.org/2019/01/17/generation-z-looks-a-lot-like-millennials-on-key-social-and-political-issues/ (retrieved May 6, 2019)

89. Parker, Kim, Nikki Graf, and Ruth Igielnik. "Generation Z Looks a Lot Like Millennials on Key Social and Political Issues." Pew Research Center, January 17, 2019. https://www.pewsocialtrends.org/2019/01/17/generation-z-looks-a-lot-like-millennials-on-key-social-and-political-issues/ (retrieved May 6, 2019)

90. Parker, Kim, Nikki Graf, and Ruth Igielnik. "Generation Z Looks a Lot Like Millennials on Key Social and Political Issues." Pew Research Center, January 17, 2019. https://www.pewsocialtrends.org/2019/01/17/generation-z-looks-a-lot-like-millennials-on-key-social-and-political-issues/ (retrieved May 6, 2019)

91. Nike.com. "Our mission is." Nike Inc. https://www.nike.com/help/a/nikeinc-mission (retrieved June 17, 2019)

92. Chick-fil-A. "Corporate Purpose." Chick-fil-A.com, accessed June 16, 2019. https://www.chick-fil-a.com/About/Who-We-Are

93. Israel, Josh. "Chick-fil-A Donated to Anti-LGBTQ Group that Bars Employees from 'Homosexual Acts.'" ThinkProgress, March 20, 2019. https://thinkprogress.org/chick-fil-a-anti-lgbtq-donations-tax-filings-62ca15281f17/ (retrieved June 16, 2019)

94. Oreo Cookie, Twitter Post, February 3, 2013, 5:48 PM, https://twitter.com/Oreo/status/298246571718483968?ref_src=twsrc%5Etfw%7Ctwcamp%5Etweetem-bed%7Ctwterm%5E298246571718483968&ref_url=https%3A%2F%2Fwww.huffpost.com%2Fentry%2Foreos-super-bowl-tweet-dunk-dark_n_2615333

95. Ives, Nat and Rupal Parekh. "Marketers Jump on Super Bowl Blackout with Real-Time Twitter Campaigns." *AdAge*, February 3, 2013. https://adage.com/article/special-report-super-bowl/marketers-jump-on-super-bowl-blackout-twitter/239575 (retrieved June 16, 2019)

96. Fromm, Jeff. "How Much Financial Influence Does Gen Z Have?" *Forbes*, January 10, 2018. https://www.forbes.com/sites/jefffromm/2018/01/10/what-you-need-to-know-about-the-financial-impact-of-gen-z-influence/#2863304a56fc (retrieved May 7, 2019)

97. Donnelly, Christopher and Renato Scaff. "Who Are the Millennial Shoppers? And What Do They Really Want?" Accenture's *Outlook*, no date. https://www.accenture.com/us-en/insight-outlook-who-are-millennial-shoppers-what-do-they-really-want-retail (retrieved June 15, 2019)

98. Alcántara, Ann-Marie. "Gen Z Has Serious Influence on Household Purchases (Even If They Aren't Buying)." *AdWeek*, September 25, 2019. https://www.adweek.com/brand-marketing/gen-z-has-serious-influence-on-household-purchases-even-if-they-arent-buying/?utm_content=lead&utm_source=postup&utm_medium=email&utm_campaign=FirstThingsFirst_Newsletter_190926054623&lyt_id=80415 (retrieved October 1, 2019)

99. Girion, Lisa. "Special Report: J&J Knew for Decades that Asbestos Lurked in Its Baby Powder." Reuters, December 14, 2018. https://www.reuters.com/article/us-johnson-johnson-cancer-special-report/special-report-jj-knew-for-decades-that-asbestos-lurked-in-its-baby-powder-idUSKBN1OD1RQ (retrieved April 28, 2019)

100. Hoffmann, Melissa. "Here Is Everything You Need to Know about the Millennial Consumer." *AdWeek*, August 13, 2014. https://www.adweek.com/digital/here-everything-you-need-know-about-millennial-consumer-159139/ (retrieved June 18, 2019)

101. Hoffmann, Melissa. "Here Is Everything You Need to Know about the Millennial Consumer." *AdWeek*, August 13, 2014. https://www.adweek.com/digital/here-everything-you-need-know-about-millennial-consumer-159139/ (retrieved June 18, 2019)

102. Patel, Deep. "10 Tips for Marketing to Gen Z." *Forbes*, March 1, 2017. https://www.forbes.com/sites/deeppatel/2017/05/01/10-tips-for-marketing-to-gen-z-consumers/#37059f113c50 (retrieved June 18, 2019)

103. Webpage. "Unemployment Statistics during the Great Depression." United States History, no date. https://www.u-s-history.com/pages/h1528.html (retrieved September 29, 2019)

104. Kane, Sally. "Common Characteristics of the Traditionalists Generation." The Balance Careers, May 2, 2019. https://www.thebalancecareers.com/workplace-characteristics-silent-generation-2164692 (retrieved September 29, 2019)

105. Kane, Sally. "Common Characteristics of the Traditionalists Generation." The Balance Careers, May 2, 2019. https://www.thebalancecareers.com/workplace-characteristics-silent-generation-2164692 (retrieved September 29, 2019)

106. Kane, Sally. "Common Characteristics of the Traditionalists Generation." The Balance Careers, May 2, 2019. https://www.thebalancecareers.com/workplace-characteristics-silent-generation-2164692 (retrieved September 29, 2019)

107. Kane, Sally. "Baby Boomers in the Workplace." The Balance Careers, April 27, 2019. https://www.thebalancecareers.com/baby-boomers-2164681 (retrieved September 29, 2019)

108. Pappas, Christopher. "8 Important Characteristics of Baby Boomers eLearning Professionals Should Know." eLearning Industry, January 29, 2016. https://elearningindustry.com/8-important-characteristics-baby-boomers-elearning-professionals-know (retrieved September 29, 2019)

109. Staff. "The Strengths and Weaknesses of Every Generation in Your Workforce." Get Smarter, January 18, 2017. https://www.getsmarter.com/blog/career-advice/know-your-generationals/ (retrieved September 29, 2019)

110. Staff. "The Strengths and Weaknesses of Every Generation in Your Workforce." Get Smarter, January 18, 2017. https://www.getsmarter.com/blog/career-advice/know-your-generationals/ (retrieved September 29, 2019)

111. Kane, Sally. "The Common Characteristics of Generation X Professionals." The Balance Careers, April 17, 2019. https://www.thebalancecareers.com/common-characteristics-of-generation-x-professionals-2164682 (retrieved September 29, 2019)

112. Carnegie, Dale. *How to Win Friends and Influence People* (New York: Simon & Schuster, 1936).

113. Carnegie, Dale. *How to Win Friends and Influence People* (New York: Simon & Schuster, 1936), 3

114. Carnegie, Dale. *How to Win Friends and Influence People* (New York: Simon & Schuster, 1936), 19

115. Carnegie, Dale. *How to Win Friends and Influence People* (New York: Simon & Schuster, 1936), 121

116. Carnegie, Dale. *How to Win Friends and Influence People* (New York: Simon & Schuster, 1936), 225

117. Carnegie, Dale. *How to Win Friends and Influence People* (New York: Simon & Schuster, 1936), 129

118. Carnegie, Dale. *How to Win Friends and Influence People* (New York: Simon & Schuster, 1936), 130

119. Website copy. "Create Your Own Tools." Snapchat, no date. https://www.snapchat.com/create (retrieved January 19, 2020)

120. Carnegie, Dale. *How to Win Friends and Influence People* (New York: Simon & Schuster, 1936), 181

121. Carnegie, Dale. *How to Win Friends and Influence People* (New York: Simon & Schuster, 1936), 187

122. Carnegie, Dale. *How to Win Friends and Influence People* (New York: Simon & Schuster, 1936), 237

123. Carnegie, Dale. *How to Win Friends and Influence People* (New York: Simon & Schuster, 1936), 241

124. Nelson, Libby. "Yale's Big Fight over Sensitivity and Free Speech, Explained." Vox, November 7, 2015. https://www.vox.com/2015/11/7/9689330/yale-halloween-email (retrieved November 3, 2019)

125. Nelson, Libby. "Yale's Big Fight over Sensitivity and Free Speech, Explained." Vox, November 7, 2015. https://www.vox.com/2015/11/7/9689330/yale-halloween-email (retrieved November 3, 2019)

126. Fry, Richard. "Millennials Projected to Overtake Baby Boomers as America's Largest Generation." Pew Research Center, March 1, 2018. https://www.pewresearch.org/fact-tank/2018/03/01/millennials-overtake-baby-boomers/ (retrieved May 27, 2019)

127. Website copy. "Her Life." National Susan B. Anthony Museum & House, no date. https://susanbanthonyhouse.org/blog/her-life/ (retrieved January 19, 2020)

128. Website copy. "Major King Events Chronology: 1929–1968." Stanford University: The Martin Luther King, Jr. Research and Education Institute, no date. https://kinginstitute.stanford.edu/king-resources/major-king-events-chronology-1929-1968 (retrieved January 19, 2020)

129. Masters, Kim. "Kim Masters: Has #MeToo Gone Too Far? No, It Hasn't Gone Far Enough." *The Hollywood Reporter*, December 12, 2019. https://www.hollywoodreporter.com/news/kim-masters-has-metoo-gone-far-no-it-hasnt-gone-far-1260429?utm_source=Sailthru&utm_medium=email&utm_campaign=THR%20Breaking%20News_2019-12-12%2007:45:00_sdrury&utm_term=hollywoodreporter_breakingnews (retrieved December 16, 2019)

130. Masters, Kim. "Kim Masters: Has #MeToo Gone Too Far? No, It Hasn't Gone Far Enough." *The Hollywood Reporter*, December 12, 2019. https://www.hollywoodreporter.com/news/kim-masters-has-metoo-gone-far-no-it-hasnt-gone-far-1260429?utm_source=Sailthru&utm_medium=email&utm_campaign=THR Breaking News_2019-12-12 07:45:00_sdrury&utm_term=hollywoodreporter_breakingnews (retrieved December 16, 2019)

131. Moniuszko, Sara M. and Cara Kelly. "Harvey Weinstein Scandal: A Complete List of the 87 Accusers." *USA Today*, October 27, 2017. https://www.usatoday.com/story/life/people/2017/10/27/weinstein-scandal-complete-list-accusers/804663001/ (retrieved February 24, 2020)

132. Paul, Deanna. "Weinstein Found Guilty of Third-Degree Rape and First-Degree Criminal Sexual Act." *Wall Street Journal*, February 24, 2020. https://www.wsj.com/articles/weinstein-convicted-of-third-degree-rape-and-first-degree-criminal-sexual-act-11582562791?mod=hp_lead_pos5 (retrieved February 24, 2020)

133. Vagianos, Alanna. "Casey Affleck Apologizes for 'Unprofessional' Behavior after Me Too Backlash." *Huff Post*, August 13, 2018. https://www.huffpost.com/entry/casey-affleck-apologizes-me-too-backlash_n_5b6c7bc6e4b0530743c81594 (retrieved November 7, 2019)

134. Singer, Jenny. "Here Are All the Famous Men Who Have Tried to Come Back from #MeToo." *The Schmooze*, April 25, 2019. https://forward.com/schmooze/420038/here-are-all-the-famous-men-who-have-tried-to-come-back-from-metoo/ (retrieved November 7, 2019)

135. American Psychiatric Association. "Personality Disorders." In Diagnostic and Statistical Manual of Mental Disorders, 5th ed. (Washington, D.C.: 2013)

136. Merrill Lynch Wealth Management. "Early Adulthood: The Pursuit of Financial Independence." New York: Bank of America Corporation, 2019. https://www.ml.com/early-adulthood-age-wave.html (retrieved April 23, 2019)

137. *Encyclopedia Britannica*, s.v. J-Curve Hypothesis," by John J. Jost and Avital Mentovich, accessed April 19, 2019, https://www.britannica.com/topic/J-curve-hypothesis

138. Budson, Andrew E. "Don't Listen to Your Lizard Brain." *Psychology Today*, December 3, 2017. https://www.psychologytoday.com/us/blog/managing-your-memory/201712/don-t-listen-your-lizard-brain (retrieved April 21, 2019)

139. Ryback, Ralph. "Why We Resist Change." *Psychology Today*, January 25, 2017. https://www.psychologytoday.com/us/blog/the-truisms-wellness/201701/why-we-resist-change (retrieved April 21, 2019)

140. The Dalai Lama. *The Art of Happiness: 10th Anniversary Edition.* (New York: Penguin Group, 1998), p. 193.

141. Fry, Richard. "For First Time in Modern Era, Living with Parents Edges out Other Living Arrangements for 18- to 34-Year-Olds." Pew Research Center's Social & Demographic Trends, June 10, 2016. https://www.pewsocialtrends.org/2016/05/24/for-first-time-in-modern-era-living-with-parents-edges-out-other-living-arrangements-for-18-to-34-year-olds/ (retrieved April 18, 2019)

142. Liu, Evie. "Why Won't Millennials Embrace the Stock Market." *Barron's*, July 31, 2017. https://www.barrons.com/articles/why-wont-millennials-embrace-the-stock-market-1501533989 (retrieved June 17, 2019)

143. Merrill Lynch Wealth Management. "Early Adulthood: The Pursuit of Financial Independence." New York: Bank of America Corporation, 2019. https://www.ml.com/early-adulthood-age-wave.html (retrieved April 23, 2019)

144. Lewis, Katherine Reynolds. "Everything You Need to Know about Your Millennial Co-Workers." *Fortune*, June 23, 2015. http://fortune.com/2015/06/23/know-your-millennial-co-workers/ (retrieved June 18, 2019)

145. Stahl, Ashley. "Gen Z: What to Expect from the New Workforce." *Forbes*, September 26, 2018. https://www.forbes.com/sites/ashleystahl/2018/09/26/gen-z-what-to-expect-from-the-new-work-force/#5d5f00863e05 (retrieved June 15, 2019)

146. Adamy, Janet. "Gen Z Is Coming to Your Office. Get Ready to Adapt." *The Wall Street Journal*, September 06, 2018. https://www.wsj.com/graphics/genz-is-coming-to-your-office/ (retrieved June 15, 2019)

147. Fry, Richard. "Millennials Are the Largest Generation in the U.S. Labor Force." Pew Research Center, April 11, 2018. https://www.pewresearch.org/fact-tank/2018/04/11/millennials-largest-generation-us-labor-force/ (retrieved June 16, 2019)

148. Levin, Dan. "Generation Z: Who They Are, in Their Own Words." The *New York Times*, March 28, 2019. https://www.nytimes.com/2019/03/28/us/gen-z-in-their-words.html (retrieved June 16, 2019)

149. Williams, Alex. "Meet Alpha: The Next 'Next Generation.'" The *New York Times*, September 19, 2015. https://www.nytimes.com/2015/09/19/fashion/meet-alpha-the-next-next-generation.html?_r=0 (retrieved June 15, 2019)

150. Hoffower, Hillary. "7 Ways Millennials Are Changing Marriage, from Signing Prenups to Staying Together Longer than Past Generations." *Business Insider*, May 24, 2019. https://www.businessinsider.com/how-millennials-are-changing-marriage-divorce-weddings-prenups-2019-5 (retrieved June 15, 2019)

151. Newman, Susan. "Should We Worry about Millennials Not Having Babies?" *Psychology Today*, April 25, 2018. https://www.psychologytoday.com/us/blog/singletons/201804/should-we-worry-about-millennials-not-having-babies (retrieved June 15, 2019)

152. Vargason, Derrick. "Meet Generation Alpha: 3 Things Educators Should Know." NWEA Blog, November 16, 2017. https://www.nwea.org/blog/2017/meet-generation-alpha-3-things-educators-know/# (retrieved June 15, 2019)

153. Business Insider. "Generation Z: Latest Characteristics, Research and Facts." *Business Insider*, no date. https://www.businessinsider.com/generation-z (retrieved May 27, 2019)

154. Pasquarelli, Adrianne, and E.J. Schultz. "Move Over Gen Z, Generation Alpha Is the One to Watch." *AdAge*, January 22, 2019. https://adage.com/article/cmo-strategy/move-gen-z-generation-alpha-watch/316314 (retrieved June 15, 2019)

155. Seppälä, Emma and Kim Cameron. "Proof That Positive Work Cultures Are More Productive." *Harvard Business Review*, December 1, 2015. https://hbr.org/2015/12/proof-that-positive-work-cultures-are-more-productive (retrieved September 9, 2019)

156. Meister, Jeanne C. "Survey: What Employees Want Most from Their Workspaces." *Harvard Business Review*, August 26, 2019. https://hbr.org/2019/08/survey-what-employees-want-most-from-their-workspaces (retrieved September 27, 2019)

157. Meister, Jeanne C. "Survey: What Employees Want Most from Their Workspaces." *Harvard Business Review*, August 26, 2019. https://hbr.org/2019/08/survey-what-employees-want-most-from-their-workspaces (retrieved September 27, 2019)

158. Meister, Jeanne C. "Survey: What Employees Want Most from Their Workspaces." *Harvard Business Review*, August 26, 2019. https://hbr.org/2019/08/survey-what-employees-want-most-from-their-workspaces (retrieved September 27, 2019)

159. Staff. "Encyclopedia for Business, 2nd Edition: Stress in the Workplace." Reference for Business, no date. https://www.referenceforbusiness.com/encyclopedia/Str-The/Stress-in-the-Workplace.html (retrieved September 16, 2019)

160. Goldschein, Eric and Kim Bhasin. "14 Surprising Ways Employees Cost Their Companies Billions in the Workplace." *Business Insider*, November 29, 2011. https://www.businessinsider.com/surprising-costs-to-the-work-place-2011-11?op=1#lost-productivity-due-to-insomnia-costs-companies-3156-per-employee-1 (retrieved September 16, 2019)

161. Staff. "The WBI Definition of Workplace Bullying." Workplace Bullying Institute, no date. https://www.workplacebullying.org/individuals/problem/definition/ (retrieved September 16, 2019)

162. Goldschein, Eric and Kim Bhasin. "14 Surprising Ways Employees Cost Their Companies Billions in the Workplace." *Business Insider*, November 29, 2011. https://www.businessinsider.com/surprising-costs-to-the-work-place-2011-11?op=1#lost-productivity-due-to-insomnia-costs-companies-3156-per-employee-1 (retrieved September 16, 2019)

163. Goldschein, Eric and Kim Bhasin. "14 Surprising Ways Employees Cost Their Companies Billions in the Workplace." *Business Insider*, November 29, 2011. https://www.businessinsider.com/surprising-costs-to-the-work-place-2011-11?op=1#lost-productivity-due-to-insomnia-costs-companies-3156-per-employee-1 (retrieved September 16, 2019)

164. Amy Adkins. "Millennials: The Job-Hopping Generation." Gallup, no date. https://www.gallup.com/workplace/231587/millennials-job-hopping-generation.aspx (retrieved September 16, 2019)

165. Survey. "Millennials Are Most Likely to Stay Loyal to Jobs with Development Opportunities." Instructure Press Release, July 18, 2018. https://www.instructure.com/bridge/news/press-releases/millennials-are-most-likely-stay-loyal-jobs-development-opportunities?newhome=bridge (retrieved September 16, 2019)

166. Stillman, David and Jonah Stillman. "Move Over, Millennials; Generation Z Is Here." The Society for Human Resource Management, April 11, 2017. https://www.shrm.org/resourcesandtools/hr-topics/behavioral-competencies/global-and-cultural-effectiveness/pages/move-over-millennials-generation-z-is-here.aspx (retrieved September 17, 2019)

167. Ho, Benjamin and Caroline Pham. "Insight: Generation Z—What Employers Can Expect with the Next Generation of Workers." *Bloomberg Law*, August 8, 2019. https://news.bloomberglaw.com/daily-labor-report/insight-generation-z-what-employers-can-expect-with-the-next-generation-of-workers (retrieved September 16, 2019)

168. Wingard, Jason. "Reverse Mentoring: 3 Proven Outcomes Driving Change." *Forbes*, August 8, 2018. https://www.forbes.com/sites/jasonwingard/2018/08/08/reverse-mentoring-3-proven-outcomes-driving-change/#55e543a18b51 (retrieved October 1, 2019)

169. Staff Report. "The Voice of Generation Z—What Post-Millennials Are Saying about Work." Rainmaker Thinking, 2018. http://rainmakerthinking.com/wp-content/uploads/2018/09/THE-VOICE-OF-GENERATION-Z_Final.pdf (retrieved September 17, 2019)

170. Merrill Lynch Wealth Management. "Early Adulthood: The Pursuit of Financial Independence." New York: Bank of America Corporation, 2019. https://www.ml.com/early-adulthood-age-wave.html (retrieved April 23, 2019)

171. Piper Jaffray & Co. "Piper Jaffray 37th Semi-Annual Taking Stock with Teens® Survey, Spring 2019." Piper Jaffray & Co., April 2019. http://www.piperjaffray.com/private/pdf/CM-19-0338%20TSWT%20Infographic%20Spring%202019_11x17.pdf (retrieved September 9, 2019)

172. Piper Jaffray & Co. "Piper Jaffray 37th Semi-Annual Taking Stock with Teens® Survey, Spring 2019." Piper Jaffray & Co., April 2019. http://www.piperjaffray.com/private/pdf/CM-19-0338%20TSWT%20Infographic%20Spring%202019_11x17.pdf (retrieved September 9, 2019)

173. Lybarger, Jeremy. "Why Walmart Became LGBT-Friendly." *Advocate*, August 31, 2016. https://www.advocate.com/politics/2016/8/31/why-walmart-became-lgbt-friendly (retrieved November 7, 2019)

174. CBS News/Associated Press. "Will Walmart's Decision to Stop Selling Some Ammo Reduce Guns on the Street?" *CBS News*, September 4, 2019. https://www.cbsnews.com/news/will-walmarts-decision-to-stop-selling-some-ammo-help-reduce-guns/ (retrieved November 7, 2019)

175. Bloom, David. "How Gen Z and Millennials Are Reshaping What Power Is, and What It Means for Brands." *Forbes*, September 12, 2019. https://www.forbes.com/sites/dbloom/2019/09/12/how-gen-z-and-millennials-are-reshaping-what-power-is-and-what-it-means-for-brands/#bcb06316d9f4 (retrieved September 27, 2019)

176. Edgers, Geoff. "Roseanne Barr Just Can't Shut Up." The *Washington Post*, March 21, 2019. https://www.washingtonpost.com/news/style/wp/2019/03/21/feature/inside-roseanne-barrs-explosive-tweet/ (retrieved September 24, 2019)

177. Fleming, Mike. "Morgan Spurlock on the Super-Size #MeToo Life Lessons Learned after His Voluntary Trip down the Rabbit Hole." *Deadline Hollywood*, September 23, 2019 https://deadline.com/2019/09/morgan-spurlock-super-size-me-holy-chicken-controversial-essay-interview-1202742387/ (retrieved September 23, 2019)

178. Mayer, Jane. "The Case of Al Franken." *The New Yorker*, July 22, 2019. https://www.newyorker.com/magazine/2019/07/29/the-case-of-al-franken (retrieved September 25, 2019)

179. Nakamura, Reid. "'Survivor' Contestant Kellee Kim Addresses Dan Spilo Ouster at Finale Reunion: 'I Was Not Being Supported or Believed.'" *The Wrap*, December 18, 2019. https://www.thewrap.com/survivor-contestant-kellee-kim-addresses-dan-spilo-ouster-at-finale-reunion-i-was-not-being-supported-or-believed/ (retrieved January 6, 2020)

180. Nakamura, Reid. "'Survivor' Contestant Kellee Kim Addresses Dan Spilo Ouster at Finale Reunion: 'I Was Not Being Supported or Believed.'" *The Wrap*, December 18, 2019. https://www.thewrap.com/survivor-contestant-kellee-kim-addresses-dan-spilo-ouster-at-finale-reunion-i-was-not-being-supported-or-believed/ (retrieved January 6, 2020)

181. DOJ Justice Manual. "262. Polygraphs—Introduction at Trial." United States Department of Justice, no date. https://www.justice.gov/jm/criminal-resource-manual-262-polygraphs-introduction-trial (retrieved September 26, 2019)

182. Legal Information Institute. "U.S. Constitution Annotated>Amendment V>Due Process>History and Scope." Cornell Law School, no date. https://www.law.cornell.edu/constitution-conan/amendment-5/history-and-scope (retrieved September 26, 2019)

183. Website copy. "What Is RULER: The RULER Skills." Yale University, Rulerapproach.org, no date. https://www.rulerapproach.org/about/what-is-ruler/ (retrieved September 26, 2019)

184. Clarke, Tara. "The Dot-Com Crash of 2000–2002." *Money Morning*, June 12, 2015. https://moneymorning.com/2015/06/12/the-dot-com-crash-of-2000-2002/ (Retrieved January 30, 2020)

Published by

TVGUESTPERT PUBLISHING

JACK H. HARRIS
Father of the Blob: The Making
of a Monster Smash and Other
Hollywood Tales
Paperback: $16.95
Kindle/Nook: $9.99

New York Times Best Seller
CHRISTY WHITMAN
The Art of Having It
All: A Woman's Guide to
Unlimited Abundance
Paperback: $16.95
Kindle/Nook: $9.99
Audible Book: $13.00

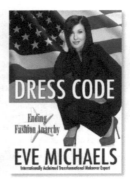

EVE MICHAELS
Dress Code: Ending
Fashion Anarchy
Paperback: $15.95
Kindle/Nook: $9.99
Audible Book: $17.95

IAN WINER
Ubiquitous Relativity: My
Truth is Not the Truth
Paperback: $16.95
Kindle: $9.99

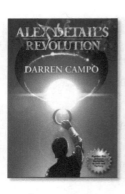

DARREN CAMPO
Alex Detail's Revolution
Paperback: $9.95
Hardcover: $22.95
Kindle: $9.15

DARREN CAMPO
Alex Detail's Rebellion
Hardcover: $22.95
Kindle: $9.99

DARREN CAMPO
Disappearing Spell:
Generationist Files:
Book 1
Kindle: $2.99

DARREN CAMPO
Stingers
Paperback: $9.99
Kindle: $9.99

TVGuestpert Publishing
11664 National Blvd, #345
Los Angeles, CA. 90064
310-584-1504
www.TVGPublishing.com

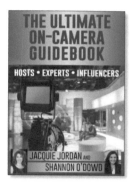

JACQUIE JORDAN AND
SHANNON O'DOWD
*The Ultimate On-
Camera Guidebook:
Hosts*Experts*Influencers*
Paperback: $16.95
Kindle: $9.99

JACQUIE JORDAN
*Heartfelt Marketing:
Allowing the Universe to Be
Your Business Partner*
Paperback: $15.95
Kindle: $9.99
Audible: $9.95

JACQUIE JORDAN
*Get on TV! The Insider's
Guide to Pitching the
Producers and Promoting
Yourself*
Published by Sourcebooks
Paperback: $14.95
Kindle: $9.99
Nook: $14.95

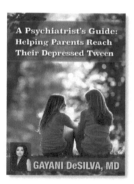

GAYANI DESILVA, MD
*A Psychiatrist's Guide: Helping
Parents Reach Their Depressed
Tween*
Paperback: $16.95
Kindle: $9.99

GAYANI DESILVA, MD
*A Psychiatrist's Guide: Stop
Teen Addiction Before It Starts*
Paperback: $16.95
Audible: $14.95
Kindle: $9.99

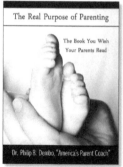

DR. PHILIP DEMBO
*The Real Purpose of
Parenting: The Book You Wish
Your Parents Read*
Paperback: $15.95
Kindle: $9.99
Audible: $23.95